DEDICATION

Had this dedication been written two years ago, there would be only one dedicatory subject, Devi, my wife of 59 years and the love of my life. On December 28, 2022, Devi passed away and everything changed. My life changed. My future changed. Today is different. I am forced to look elsewhere for family and friends who now fill that spot. Fortunately, the choice is easy, and the candidates are few, my two children, Trina Titus Lozano and my son, Aaron Titus. They fill my life with more joy, happiness and sheer pride than anyone deserves to have in this life.

The foundation to our relationship, however, goes deeper than the DNA mutually inherited from their mother and me. It is rooted and grounded in our relationship to Jesus Christ, an unbreakable cord that binds us together in a love that transcends all familial fidelity or earthly explanation. I will spend eternity thanking my Lord and Savior, Jesus Christ, who has blessed our family beyond anything any of us could have imagined. It is Christ, and Christ alone, who is the foundation to everything we are and do. I dedicate this book my daughter, my son and my Lord. My gratitude will span eternity, and we will follow the Lamb wherever He goes.

Larry

THE ACCESS TO POWER

TEN KINGDOM KEYS TO IGNITE
EVANGELISM AND REVIVE THE
CHURCH

FOREWORD BY KENNETH C. ULMER

I am facing initiation into the often maligned yet more often relished octogenarian fraternity. I have recently entered the transition season of being retired – or rather, "re-positioned" as several of my colleagues label the post-pastoral assignments of local church ministry. As I reflect on over four decades of realizing the daunting prophetic announcement by a graduate school of theology professor: "Sunday comes around every seven days", I find myself being both obsessed and distressed by the future of the church. My concern comes from a synthesis of a personal disdain and a spiritual discernment.

I hate waiting in airports! I acknowledge this character flaw that shamelessly reveals a lack of the fruit of the spirit: patience; only one lack among many remaining areas of spiritual growth in my six decades of salvation. After landing in a small midwestern town to speak at a revival in a small African American Baptist church, I made my way from the arrival gate to the baggage area amid the dozens of other travelers. I arrived at the carousel which was supposed to contain my luggage. Fellow travelers continued to walk past me with their retrieved bags making their way to the exit. I was told there would be someone there to pick me up. However, I saw no one who approached me as my designated driver. The throng of travelers with retrieved luggage began to dwindle. No driver. A remaining few travelers occupied the baggage area, but no one seemed to be looking for an African American boy from California. The hustle and bustle subsided leaving only a lingering traveler, a couple of airport workers and me – but no driver. After almost thirty torturous minutes for frustration, there was only me and one other elderly guy in the baggage area. As I paced back and forth in my long-gone pseudo-patience, the singular guy sitting near the carousel, made his way slowly to me and gingerly said, "are you Rev. Uhhlma?" I said, "yes sir." He sheepishly smiled and said, "aww, Reverend I been her almost an hour waiting for you; I must have passed you a dozen times." I really was not amused at this confusion. Then he reached into his inside coat pocket and said, "Reverend, I'm so sorry; but sir, I didn't recognize you." He showed me the picture in his hand and with a crooked smile, he said, "I'm sorry Reverend, but you don't look like your picture. See look." And sure enough my office had sent him an old picture of me with a huge afro, a wide tie that almost covered my neck and a loud plaid suit with absolutely no class or style. The old gentleman said, I passed you by and didn't recognize you because you don't look like your picture.

I fear the world is passing by the church – the Body of Christ, the Spirit-filled incarnation of the resurrected and reigning King of Kings – passing right by, because the church doesn't look like its picture – the picture in the Bible of a world changing, life changing, empowering representation of the Living Lord. We don't look like our picture.

Larry Titus responds to the haunting daunting query raised by the psalmist: "When the foundations are being destroyed, what can the righteous do?" Ps 11:3 NIV. He speaks from several perspectives. His is a powerful poignant prophetic voice. He brings the heart of a passionate pastor and the paternal sensitivity of one who has been spiritual father to countless national and global leaders. This project is grounded in the conviction that most will do better when they know better.

With the wisdom of a skilled worker, he begins with the biblical foundation of the ecclesiastical offices of Apostles and prophets. These foundational gifts to the church which have often been exploited, exaggerated or eliminated become the foundation for the kingdom structure of the church. In the spirit of the old musical gospel invitation: "now let us all go back to the old landmark" Titus challenges the reader to acknowledge and affirm these present-day offices as the foundation of the Kingdom community.

He highlights the way the church has flip-flopped the commission of our Lord. Our clarion call is "come": come to my church, come hear my preacher, come hear my choir. When in fact we are called and commissioned to "go" – "go make disciples"; a call and journey that goes far beyond our neighborhood and local community. Making disciples is boundary-less. It begins in Jerusalem, where they were. When it goes to Judea, it crosses, geographical boundaries. When it goes to Samaria, it crosses racial and cultural boundaries. When the message of the life changing Gospel of Jesus Christ targets the uttermost parts of the world, the nations, it crosses all global boundaries, all ethnicities. All of this is to be done through the empowerment and equipping of gifted soldiers in the army of the Lord. This is the work of the ministry.

With a keen eye for the subtleties of drifting away from the pillars and ground of truth, he re-emphasizes a seemingly lost dynamic of the contemporary emphasis on "diversity". He highlights generational diversity with the exhortation to focus of the next and coming generation of youth – that is already here! He suggests a return to the simplistic fundamental exhortation that we ought always to pray! It is an echo of a once popular ecclesiastical cliché: much prayer, much power; little prayer little power; no prayer, no power! This being the marching mandate of a praying church continually seeking discernment, wisdom and more and more of the power of the Holy Spirit. He will later challenge us to prayerfully pray in the pattern of the early church, with the expectation of the biblical promise of signs, wonders and miracles that follow through the power of promise of the Holy Spirit.

This work is a gentle but firm exhortation to intentionally and courageously focus the proclamation of the word on building the Kingdom. Such a timely word for those of us who have strenuously preached to build our local congregations and fill our local gathering places, often at the neglect of the Kingdom mandate. This will become both a biblical reminder and a revised homiletic agenda to a generation of pulpiteers whose models and examples have been a former generational target on bigger buildings, bigger budgets and bigger numbers of pew occupants.

With a painful plea Titus recalls and recalls us to the plaintive petition of our Lord to the Father to "make us one." In a world where the church is as, or more divided than the world, he calls for a reemphasis on Christological unity. This is the unity for which our Lord prayed and that was demonstrated – making it possible – in the first church at Pentecost and the church at Ephesus.

Titus provides an expansion of Eugene Peterson's excellent contemporary description of the essence of Christian ministry. In his paraphrased version The Message, Peterson pictures ministry in theatrical terms: "It seems to me that God has put us who bear his Message on stage in a theater in which no one wants to buy a ticket." (1 Cor 4:9 from THE MESSAGE: The Bible in Contemporary Language © 2002 by Eugene H. Peterson. All rights reserved.) Titus and Peterson go on to tell us which roles we play on the stage of ministry life. "We are servants of Christ" 1 Cor 4:1(from THE MESSAGE: The Bible in

Contemporary Language © 2002 by Eugene H. Peterson. All rights reserved.) He calls leaders to lead in the role of servants. What a refreshing call and challenge to a generation that seems to have emphasized being high ranking master generals rather than humble servant leaders.

Titus concludes with the foundational reminder to follow the example of Paul: that we know nothing except Jesus Christ and Him crucified. Preach Jesus! Let the church again look like the church to those travelers who are tempted to walk past us.

As a veteran of four decades of spiritual warfare I can attest that preaching Jesus will often get you into trouble. But preaching that same Jesus will get you out of trouble. This is a foundational truth. What shall we do when our foundations are destroyed? PREACH JESUS as servants of the highest, in the power of the Holy Spirit and unity of the Body of Christ to generations yet coming as we make disciples equipped in their gifts grounded on the foundation of apostolic and prophetic anointing – all bathed in continuous prayer! Let His Kingdom come. Let His will be done.

Kenneth C. Ulmer, PhD, DMin.
Presiding Bishop
Macedonia International Bible Fellowship

THE ACCESS TO POWER

TEN KINGDOM KEYS TO IGNITE EVANGELISM AND REVIVE THE CHURCH

LARRY TITUS

Five
Stones
Press

COPYRIGHT

CONTENTS

THE ACCESS TO POWER

TEN KINGDOM KEYS TO IGNITE
EVANGELISM AND REVIVE THE
CHURCH

INTRODUCTION

On a spring morning in May of 1969, the Lord began to share with me truths concerning the kingdom of God and how it relates to His church on earth. Until then, my understanding of God's purpose for the church was to build a bigger building, promote my program, preach better sermons, have more people attend Sunday services, and increase our budget through tithes and offerings. Of course, evangelism and missions were also part of the mix, but not in any concerted effort.

My encounter with the Lord changed the course of my entire ministry from that day forward until today. I shifted my entire focus from:

- being church oriented *to* kingdom oriented
- building bigger congregations *to* taking cities, states, and nations for Jesus

- preaching better sermons *to* witnessing the powers and principalities of hell put under the feet of the church
- spending money on us *to* resourcing global leaders and investing in world-changers.

Kingdom Glasses

I removed my "church" glasses and put on "kingdom" glasses. I noticed the sparsity of Jesus' teaching as regards the church, which He mentioned only twice in Matthew 16:18 and Matthew 18:17. Conversely, He spoke on the kingdom of God over one hundred times in the Gospels.

I noted that most of Jesus' teaching related to the kingdom of God, including nearly all His parables. I was intrigued to discover that His first and last sermons were on the kingdom of God. I was equally surprised to learn that He preached on the kingdom of God in every town He visited, then sent out the Twelve and the seventy-two to do likewise (Matthew 4:23; 9:35, Luke 4:43; 10:1).

Since Jesus appears to have had only one message in His repertoire, it is doubtful that most churches would have invited Him back more than once or twice. "Don't you have another message you could preach? We've already heard this one eight times."

The kingdom began when King Jesus appeared on this earth and will continue until all enemies are put under His feet upon His second return (1 Corinthians 15:25). Jesus' activity on earth underscored the message of the kingdom of God, and the subsequent damage to the kingdom of darkness was immediate and astronomical.

Every miracle was a prelude and invitation to enter the kingdom of heaven.

Every demoniac delivered caused a revolt in heaven. Jesus witnessed Satan fall as swiftly as a bolt of lightning rips through the sky (Luke 10:18).

Every person born again was instantly ushered into the kingdom of God and delivered from the dominion and authority of darkness.

The poor were delivered from the bondage of poverty and set free to liberty and life in Christ Jesus.

Greetings, Church! Welcome to the Building

As I pondered the purpose of the church in the kingdom of God, I had a second epiphany. The church, or in Greek, the *ekklesia* of God, is not a building, a program, an institution, or a place to go to on Sunday. Instead, it is the living, vibrant organism called the body of Christ, with Jesus as the Head (Ephesians 1:22–23). That opened further revelation. If the kingdoms of darkness are under the feet of Jesus, who are the feet? The church, His body, of course. Everything Jesus was in the world, we are. We, the church, are an extension of the hands, feet, voice, anointing, and authority of Jesus. We are His, a building not made with hands (2 Corinthians 5:1).

This revelation changed everything in my practical theology. I could no longer invite people to the church building but to Jesus, the Head of the church. In obedience to this revelation, Devi, my wife and I began going to the streets, parks, drug dens, and bars with the message of Jesus and His kingdom. The kingdom's announcement included salvation, healing, and deliverance. Thousands of youths responded to the message. It was a "go" gospel, not a "come" gospel. God took the church out of the church building so we could be the true building of God, the body of Christ. When you gather, it is not a witticism to say, "Greetings, church! Welcome to the building;" it is scriptural.

Jesus taught us to pray for the Father's kingdom to come and then promised *"all these things"* to come because we see it as our priority (Matthew 6:33).

Powerful Access

Recently, I began to ponder what it meant when Jesus said He would give the keys of the kingdom to the church. Take note that in Matthew 16:19, Jesus does not give us the keys to the church but to the kingdom of heaven. To clarify, Jesus said that the church belonged to Him and that He would build it.

Practically speaking, keys have tremendous power because they grant access. With a key, we lock and unlock our cars, homes, and buildings; everything locked inside is accessible to the one who holds the key. Therefore, when the Head of the church, Jesus, gives multiple keys to the church, imagine the power of access.

These keys, *plural,* are mentioned twice in the New Testament, first in Matthew 16:19: *"And I will give you the keys to the **kingdom of heaven**,"* (NIV) and second in Revelation 1:17–18: *"I [Jesus] died, and behold I am alive forevermore, and I have the keys of **Death and Hades**."**

---

* All Scripture references are from the ESV translation unless otherwise noted.

These powerful kingdom keys, found in Matthew 16:18, inform us that the gates of Hades, meaning Satan's dominion, cannot stand against the church that has been given the keys.

The power of a solitary key is evidenced in Revelation 20:1. One angel seizes Satan, the ancient dragon, binds him with a great chain, and casts him into the Abyss for a thousand years. Just imagine what multiple keys could do.

It seems logical that if the church understood the power of kingdom keys, they would devastate the kingdoms of darkness, put the enemy under its feet, and establish the kingdom of God. Yet we continue trying to build the church, which Jesus said was **His** possession that **He** would build, and neglect building the kingdom of God, which is **our** responsibility to build. And so, I ask…

What are these keys?

Can the keys be identified in the Bible?

Are the keys to the kingdom the same globally, or do they change according to cultures, regions, religions, or satanic strongholds?

Do the keys have physical as well as spiritual ramifications?

Ten Keys to Global Evangelism

After decades of *"seeking first the kingdom and his righteousness"* (Matthew 6:33) and hours of prayer, asking the Father what His priorities were, I felt the Lord directing me to identify Ten Kingdom Keys to Global Evangelism, hence the purpose and title of this book. I'm not suggesting these are the only keys, nor are they necessarily the ones you need to reach your city, state, and nation with the gospel. These are the keys I feel are both biblically sound and spiritually necessary to reach the world.

I'm consumed with the words of Jesus: *"And this gospel of the kingdom will be proclaimed throughout the whole world as a testimony to all nations, and then the end will come"* (Matthew 24:14 NIV).

If this gospel of the kingdom is to be preached in the whole world before Jesus returns, I feel obligated to share with you the keys that I believe are necessary to accomplish the task.

These are the keys I will be discussing at length in this book:

10 KINGDOM KEYS TO GLOBAL EVANGELISM

BUILD ON APOSTLES AND PROPHETS
EPHESIANS 2:20 | 1 CORINTHIANS 12:28

PREACH THE KINGDOM OF GOD
MATTHEW 10:7 | MATTHEW 24:14

MAKE DISCIPLES OF ALL NATIONS
MATTHEW 10:1 | MATTHEW 28:18-19

PURSUE UNITY IN THE BODY OF CHRIST
JOHN 17:21 | EPHESIANS 4:3,6,13

RELEASE PEOPLE IN THEIR GIFTS
JOHN 15:16 | ROMANS 12:4-8

BECOME A SERVANT
PHILIPPIANS 2:7 | LUKE 22:26-27

PRAY AT ALL TIMES
ACTS 1:14 | EPHESIANS 6:18

CONTEND FOR THE MIRACULOUS
ACTS 5:12 | LUKE 10:9

CONCENTRATE ON YOUTH
JOEL 2:28 | ACTS 2:17

PREACH JESUS
JOHN 12:32 | 1 CORINTHIANS 1:23

AND THIS GOSPEL OF THE KINGDOM WILL BE PREACHED IN THE WHOLE WORLD AS TESTIMONY TO ALL NATIONS, AND THEN THE END WILL COME. MATTHEW 24:14 NIV

I will expound on these points in depth in the following pages. Upon reading, consider sharing this book, or truths from this book, with others. We must change how we do things, or Christianity in the United States will be relegated to history books.

Again, I am consumed with reaching the world for Jesus and His kingdom. Will you join me?

CHAPTER 1
BUILD ON APOSTLES AND PROPHETS

"And God has placed in the church first of all apostles, second prophets" (1 Corinthians 12:28 NIV).

"Built on the foundation of the apostles and prophets, with Christ Jesus himself as the chief cornerstone" (Ephesians 2:20 NIV).

I doubt anyone reading this book hasn't been burned out, disillusioned, deluded, disgusted, disappointed, betrayed, or even worse, controlled by self-proclaimed apostles and prophets at some point in their spiritual journey. Anecdotes abound regarding such people and range from the absurd to the abusive.

In recent years, there has been a proliferation of people professing to hold one of these ascension gifts, leaving us pondering whether such claims are genuine or fraudulent. Others are convinced that apostles and prophets haven't existed since the first century, so why bother addressing the topic?

Does the Church Still Need Apostles and Prophets?

Allow me to answer emphatically: Yes! Not only are genuine apostles and prophets necessary but the American church is destined for failure without them.

The word apostle means *sent*, implying a sender or one who calls the apostle into action. However, in every nation, there are self-appointed, self-promoted, self-ordained apostles who were never called or sent. In Revelation 2:2, the Ephesian church is commended for judging false apostles, and we might want to follow their example.

The word *prophet* means *to proclaim* a message from God. As with self-appointed apostles, false prophets abound. Multiple verses in the Old and New Testaments identify false prophets and pronounce a curse on them. They ran, but God didn't send them; they prophesied, but it wasn't God. They manipulated people for their own good and deliberately deceived the innocent. False prophecies caused people to think the message was of God, and the results were devastating.

Much of what people call prophecy is grounded in witchcraft, whose primary focus is on exercising control. A false prophet aims to retain power and control over others rather than release it. I can assure you that whether God judges these so-called prophets in this life or the next, the time is coming when they will be judged for their false prophecies and self-promotional prognostications.

That said, false and fraudulent apostles and prophets parading as voices for the church in no way negate the real offices of apostles and prophets but rather enhance them.

Counterfeit money makes valid the real. Shadows prove the presence of the true object. Pretenders portend the real.

I have had more than my share of people prophesying words over me that were manufactured from their minds rather than the unction of the Holy Spirit. In most cases, I discerned a pure but misguided motive. I've also had words of wisdom, knowledge, and prophetic words for Devi and me that came straight from God's heart. Discerning the difference depends on whether the prophetic word controls or releases you. Remember, self-control—not "other" control— is the only control we have been given in the Bible (2 Timothy 1:7, Galatians 5:22–23). Isaiah 55:12 states that God's people *"shall go out in joy and be led forth in peace"*. If the prophetic word has not produced joy or peace, it's not from God.

And so, the proverbial bathwater metaphor might be appropriate here. Take, judge, and extract what is true from what is false, but don't discard the whole because of the few. Paul's words in 1 Corinthians 14:39 bear repeating: *"So, my brothers, earnestly desire to prophesy, and do not forbid speaking in tongues"*. Further, his words in 1 Thessalonians 5:20–21: *"Do not despise prophecies, but test everything; hold fast what is good."*

The Gifts of the Father, Son, and Holy Spirit

In this chapter, I want to distinguish between the ministry of apostles and prophets versus the charismatic gifts associated with them, such as prophecy, words of knowledge, wisdom, etc. There is often confusion surrounding the gifts of God, but the Bible is clear. Our triune God only gives perfect gifts (James 1:17) and imparts them as follows:

Romans 12:6–8, Father God bestows the grace gifts of prophecy, service, teaching, exhortation, generosity, leading, and acts of mercy. These gifts *"differ according to the grace given to us"* (Romans 12:6). Once you have been given a gift from God, it is irrevocable (Romans 11:29), meaning God will not remove it from your life. The gift is an integral part of you; as such, it is essential to use it for God's glory and not your own.

Ephesians 4:11, the Lord Jesus gives gifts of apostles, prophets, evangelists, shepherds, and teachers. These are called the ascension gifts (more on this in a moment) or the fivefold gifts. Jesus held, and holds, all five: Christ as apostle (Hebrews 3:1), prophet (John 6:14), evangelist (Mark 1:14), shepherd (John 10:11), and teacher (John 13:13).

1 Corinthians 12:7–11, the Holy Spirit gives "manifestation" gifts: wisdom, utterance of knowledge, faith, gifts of healing, miracles, prophecy, discernment, tongues, and interpretation. These gifts are available to every believer and manifest as the Holy Spirit desires for the edification of self and others. For example, if the Holy Spirit gives you prophetic encouragement for someone, *it does not necessarily mean you are a prophet*. You may have been given the gift from Him for the moment.

At all times, love undergirds the gifts. This means that even if you have a word for somebody that is spot on, love will often hold its tongue. We should never put our right to be right above relationships. Otherwise, we are in danger of becoming a clanging gong (1 Corinthians 13), and I cannot imagine anything more annoying than that, can you?

The Ascension Gifts of Jesus

When Jesus ascended to the Father, He gave gifts to men of the church. (The Greek word for *men* is *anthropoi*, meaning men or women). Paul penned the words of Ephesians 4:8: *"He [Jesus] gave gifts to men,"* while quoting Psalm 68:18. However, he changed the words *"receiving gifts from men"* to *"he [Jesus] gave gifts to men."* That simple preposition creates a significant change; what was Paul's logic?

When kings of antiquity won a victory, they required captives to bring gifts to their captors, as seen in the Old Testament. However, when Jesus won the victory at the cross and ascended to the Father, He gave gifts to men, the opposite of earthly rulers who received them. As a sign of victory, the gifts Jesus gave the church were in the form of leaders. What an incredible, unmerited blessing. We need to consider our spiritual leaders as ascension gifts from Jesus, worthy of appreciation and honor. Paul suggested to Timothy that they be granted double honor. *"Let the elders who rule well be considered worthy of double honor, especially those who labor in preaching and teaching"* (1 Timothy 5:17). Allow me to add a cautionary word. I have never seen a leader worth their salt who seeks to be honored.

Apostles and Prophets: First and Second Priority

Read 1 Corinthians 12:28 carefully. *"And God has appointed in the church first apostles, second prophets, third teachers, then miracles, then gifts of healing, helping, administrating, and various kinds of tongues."*

Paul prioritizes three of the five ascension gifts of Jesus. Apostles and prophets are the church's number one and two priorities. This is the only verse in all Scripture that lists the ascension gifts according to priority. The pastor is notably absent. When Paul mentions the gifts in Ephesians 4:11, they are listed in the same order but not with numerical priority.

Ephesians 2:20 says the household of God is *"built on the foundation of the apostles and prophets, Christ Jesus himself being the cornerstone."* Again, while Paul does not use *protos*, first, or *deuteros*, second, he says these ascension gifts are the church's foundation stones, with Christ Jesus being the chief stone or the Cornerstone. Again, the word *pastor* is not mentioned.

In these three references, Paul intends to make patently clear that apostles and prophets precede the other ministries. While we may prefer traditional pastoral leadership models and harbor bias against the biblical model, Paul certainly didn't. He was quite clear in identifying who should lead the New Testament church. Apostles and prophets.

Paul then lists one more gift in his spiritual office line-up. In 1 Corinthians 12:28, teaching is mentioned in third place, then the gifts of the Spirit, followed by the serving ministries.

Please note that listing these do not indicate superiority but priority. The church was never intended by the Father to be a hierarchy. Though some of the gifts take precedence, they are all equal. The church leaders are not at the top of the pyramid but at the bottom. All foundational stones, such as apostle, prophet, and teacher, are to be laid down on the foundation of Jesus, the Chief Cornerstone. As many have pointed out, church leadership should be operated from the bottom up, not the top down.

Yet for many centuries, the church has virtually ignored four of the gifts listed in Ephesians 4:11 and made pastors the number-one priority of the church, followed by teachers, with evangelists being a distant third. Missionaries are highly regarded in most cultures, especially in the West, but no one knows where they fit in the line-up except we admire their sacrifice. They have been relegated to the needed and respected, but not highly recognized, and certainly not a priority, even though they come closer to the biblical definition of one who is "sent" than that of a pastor, evangelist, or teacher.

What About Pastors?

Let's talk about pastors. The Greek word for pastor is *poimen* (pronounced poy-MANE), which means *shepherd*. It is translated seventeen times in the King James Version as *shepherd* or *Shepherd*, with a capital *S* when referring to Jesus (1 Peter 2:25). For some unknown reason, in one verse only, Ephesians 4:11, it is translated as *pastor*. The meaning is the same: one who pastures or feeds the sheep. The problem is that most churches call their leaders by the title *Pastor* rather than *Shepherd*, as described by their call.

Through the centuries, the pastor's job, title, veneration, and recognition have virtually taken the apostle and prophet out of the line-up of priority offices and replaced them with the shepherd. While it's commendable that the shepherd, the one who feeds the sheep, would find a place in senior leadership, it is not commendable when that position eclipses and essentially displaces those biblically prioritized as foundational leaders. In Acts 13, the prophets and teachers provided the pool from which the Holy Spirit identified the apostolic. My, how things have changed. Now, we have a search committee.

I'd like to note that the pastor is the only office in the Ephesian line-up of church leaders without an earthly example. You cannot find a single individual, other than our Heavenly Shepherd in the New Testament, identified by the title pastor or shepherd. Why do we emphasize a position with so little support in the New Testament? Is it possible that tradition has eclipsed and replaced the Word of God?

The Idol of Ministry

The disproportionate emphasis on the pastoral office in the modern church has led to another significant problem directly related to this; when the church only recognizes a few professional clergy in each congregation, the priesthood of all believers is nullified. The load becomes enormous when only one or two people carry the weight of the entire congregation.

The fruit of this disproportion gives birth to an unhealthy performance culture. As one of only a few bearing the weight, the pastor believes they must up their game each week to keep the congregants amused, enlightened, equipped, strengthened, and challenged. On the weeks they think they have attained this impossible standard of perfection, they feel delighted. On the weeks they don't, they feel despondent. The once well-meaning pastor's focus can change to pleasing the congregants rather than faithfully serving them.

In worst-case scenarios, the pastor spends less and less time with their family. The children rebel, inciting the warning in Titus 1:6. The spouse feels neglected, and disharmony is born. Since the church is (un-rightly so) founded on the pastor, it now takes on an unhealthy DNA of the pastor's marriage.

The increasing pressure and weight mean they must live every moment for and at the church, and there is an expectation for others to do the same. Rather than serving God, then family, then ministry, God and ministry become one, and an idol is born. As is true with any idol, it demands to be endlessly served with zero rewards for the servant. In this environment, well-meaning volunteers are shamed into service under the guise of excellence, and burnout from this performance-based culture creates a vicious cycle easily avoided by maintaining the biblical standard.

The Priesthood of All Believers (1 Peter 2:9)

In the New Testament, everyone born again has been called into the ministry. Jesus succinctly said, *"You did not choose me, but I chose you and appointed you that you should go and bear fruit and that your fruit should abide"* (John 15:16).

The church can never reach the world when only a few gifted pastors do all the work while the people in the pew remain inactive and uninvolved. We must teach them that every believer has been deputized to do the work of the ministry, not just a few professional clergy.

In the book *Contagious Disciple Making*, author David

Watson makes the point well: "By promoting and insisting on a professional clergy, the church has limited its ability and capacity to reach the world for Christ."

We must change our mindset and set ways to reach the world.

What I find scriptural, however, is that every person in leadership, whether pastor, prophet, or apostle, should carry the heart of our Great Shepherd of the sheep, Jesus Christ. I don't believe anyone is qualified to lead the flock of God, whatever their gifts, without the love of sheep. As one man told me, he was drawn to our church because he smelled the aroma of sheep; I smelled like a shepherd. I took it as a compliment and a prerequisite for any leadership position in the body of Christ. After all, two of the greatest Old Testament leaders were shepherds. Moses and David.

In John 10:16, Jesus says, *"So there will be one flock, one shepherd."* All of us overseers and elders in the flock of Jesus are under-shepherds of the *one* true Shepherd of the sheep, Jesus Christ. He is the ultimate exemplar and prototype of all spiritual leadership. He is the only Head of the church; no earthly leader is given that title. You might be a pastor, lead elder, apostle, or prophet, but you are still not the Head. The only Head of the church is seated at the Father's right hand (Ephesians 1:19–23).

It would be wise for all of us to follow the admonition of Paul "to *care for the church of God, which he obtained with his own blood*" (Acts 20:28), knowing that fierce wolves will come in, not sparing the flock. This requires constant vigilance.

But other than Jesus, no shepherd or pastor is mentioned by name in the New Testament. On the other hand, leaders are identified by name in all other church offices. In addition to the original twelve that Jesus chose, I can name several more who were identified as apostles. Several are called prophets and teachers, and at least one, Philip, is identified as an evangelist, though Paul admonishes Timothy to do the work of an evangelist.

These are the names of those holding Ephesians 4:11 offices in the New Testament:

Apostles:

Matthias, who replaced Judas, and was counted among the Twelve (Acts 1:26)

Saul (Paul) of Tarsus (Galatians 1:1; Romans 1:1; Acts 14:14)

Barnabas (Acts 13:2; 14:14)

James, the half brother of Jesus (Galatians 1:19, 1 Corinthians 15:7)

Andronicas and Junias (Romans 16:7 NIV) (*Junias* can also be feminine, *Junia,* indicating a woman could also carry the apostolic mandate.)

Silas (1 Thessalonians 1:1; 2:6)

Timothy (1 Thessalonians 1:1; 2:6)

Two unnamed apostles (2 Corinthians 8:23)

Epaphroditus (Philippians 2:25). The word in KJV is translated as *messenger,* but the Greek word is *apostolon: apostle.* The same is in 2 Corinthians 8:23.

Prophets:

Agabus (Acts 21:10)

Judas Barsabbas (Acts 15:32). This man was rejected as a replacement for Judas Iscariot.

Silas (Acts 15:32)

Daughters of Philip (Acts 21:9)

The leaders at Antioch, Barnabas, Simeon, who was called Niger, Lucius of Cyrene, Manaen, and Saul (Acts 13:1)

Evangelists:

Philip (Acts 21:8)

Timothy: (2 Timothy 4:5)

Teachers:

Five leaders at Antioch (listed above), though the Scripture doesn't specify which ones were teachers and which were prophets (Acts 13:1)

Apollos (1 Corinthians 3:6, Acts 18:24)

Pastors:

None, nada, zero, nul, ling, jelo, cero, sifr.

This begs the question, why do we continue to build the church on non-foundational offices? What if we were to build on apostolic and prophetic foundations, as Paul has admonished, rather than pastoral ones? Would that make a difference? I contend it would.

The church in America is spiraling downward at a staggering rate. Statistics show that thousands more churches close yearly than open, and church attendance is cratering. Again, it can be traced to a lack of foundational leaders.

Furthermore, where there is church growth, generally among the megachurches, the growth is more attritional than people getting saved. People are just changing pews.

People gravitate to the greatest, fastest-growing, hottest worship, best children and youth programs, and highly charismatic speakers.

Leaders will hopefully realize that someday, people will do to their church what their church did to others. They will no longer be the hottest thing going, and people will drop them in a heartbeat. The turnaround time for church-hopping seems to be getting shorter. One staff member told me, "We cannibalized all the churches around us, and now they are cannibalizing us." In other words, they used to be the hottest church around. Thousands of people left other churches to come to them. But when a hotter church sprung up, thousands left their church.

The statistics of youth leaving the church are staggering. Well over one million youth attending church will leave within the year, which means that, of every two teens in church right now, one won't return next fall. I've heard it said multiple times, though I can't back it up with statistics, that most backsliders at one point worked either as volunteers or paid staff at a church. From personal experience, however, I can attest that people who have previously worked on a church staff are some of the most bitter and burned-out people I've ever met.

All these things suggest we take a serious look at where we, the church, are going. The church in America is in serious trouble, and we will soon look like the European church, nothing but empty church buildings and a secular society that has taken over.

Covid-19 has proven exceptionally effective in pointing out our vulnerable underside. In the past few years, I have visited multiple thousand-member churches that were formerly bustling with activity and are now nearly empty. They often have a third or less of their previous attendance. And the number of churches that have appeared for sale in real estate listings is staggering. Are you interested in purchasing a former church building? Not a problem; we have quite a selection for you.

We can no longer spend time rearranging the chairs on the deck of the *Titanic*. The ship is sinking. The largest contingent of Christian believers is now in Africa, with South America and Asia close behind.

My proposal? Let's return to the beginning of the church in Acts chapter two and start over. Let's consider building on the foundation of apostles and prophets, with Jesus as the Chief Cornerstone.

Identifiers and Releasers

True apostles and prophets are identifiers and releasers. When a church is founded on its leadership, the pastoral staff has an incredible resource from which to draw. Apostles and prophets offer a covering of accountability. They are visionaries, viewing the larger picture and being able to provide this lens to the pastor. As those sent and trained to see God's activity, they will quickly recognize congregants among the vast pool of anointed men and women God has already placed within their church who have never been identified or released in their calling. Many of these congregants already function in the marketplace, but their anointing remains unrecognized within the church walls. They sit there, week after week, underutilized, while less-gifted men and women, who are neither anointed nor called, occupy a place of prominence.

To illustrate, as a guest speaker, I have on several occasions asked a pastor who their youth leader is. The pastor will point to the young man or woman in the sanctuary, and I then draw their attention to the reality that not one teenager is standing with the designated leader. Yet, on the opposite side of the room, dozens of teens are gathered around an engaging layperson. It seems simple enough to me, with little prayer or prophecy needed. To whom are they drawn? It would be best if you, the one who they connect with were talking to the teens.

Who in your congregations gives accurate words of knowledge, wisdom, or prophetic insight in their daily interaction with people? Maybe you have a budding prophet in your midst.

Who in your church is gifted to preach, teach, perform miracles, produce mature leaders, and carry extraordinary influence in leading people to Christ and making disciples? You might have an apostle on your hands. After all, it wasn't immediately apparent that Saul of Tarsus was an apostle. Maybe someone whom you have considered irascible and incorrigible is being lined up by God to reach the nations. It wouldn't be the first time God bypassed the refined, eloquent theologian and used the shoemaker, tentmaker, and lowest of trade men and women to shake cities and nations.

Where Are the Apostles?

Perhaps even now, questions are beginning to form in your mind, such as:

- How will I know if I am an apostle or prophet?
- How do we get back to the foundation of apostles and prophets?
- What does this look like practically in my local church?

The answer begins with another question: Were you sent? To reiterate, the word *apostle* in Greek is *apostolos*, which means one who was sent. Jesus initially used it in Matthew 10:2–4 and Luke 6:13–16 when He chose the twelve disciples. As soon as the disciples (*mathetes* in Greek) were sent out, the word *disciple* changed to *apostolos*. The difference between a disciple and an apostle is that the apostle is sent.

In Matthew 10:2 and Luke 6:1, Jesus Himself is the sending agent. In the church at Antioch in Acts 13:2 and 4, the Holy Spirit is the sending agent, with the teachers and prophets identifying the ones to be sent in an atmosphere of prayer and fasting. The same pattern continues to this day. Under the direction of Jesus, the Head of the church, the Holy Spirit is the sending agent.

The Principle of Apostleship

In his work *Renewal Theology: Systematic Theology from a Charismatic Perspective*, J. Rodman Williams distinguishes between *apostleship* (Romans 1:4–5 and 1 Corinthians 9:2) and the ongoing apostolic ministry of Ephesians 4. He notes:

A distinction may be made between the foundational ministry of apostle, that is, the apostleship, and the ongoing ministry of others who are called apostles. In this broader sense an apostle is one sent, commissioned, *and therefore is not affixed to a particular location or church. He does not have the authority of a foundational apostle nor are his words equally inspired. Such an apostle operates in a translocal manner but does not operate independently. He is church based, representing a particular church, but ministering largely in a field beyond. Such apostles are always essential to the life of a church that realizes its call to reach out beyond itself in the mission of the gospel.*

In other words, while we honor and uphold the foundational office of apostleship in the New Testament, we must not negate the ongoing *ministry* of apostles who continually call the church to reach beyond parochial boundaries and into the world.

Williams continues:

*There were many in the New Testament church who preached widely, functioned as missionaries, and represented the churches in different ways. These were also apostles—and leaders like these are surely needed at **all times** in the life of the church* [emphasis added].

A key identifier in defining the role of the apostle today is to note that within the principle of apostleship, discipleship always turns into sent-ship. I'm convinced there are apostolic and prophetic ministries currently available in our pews that no one recognizes. We need to listen to the voice of the Holy Spirit to identify those whom God has chosen.

Being the leader of a megachurch doesn't necessarily qualify you as an apostle, neither does leading a small congregation disqualify you. You have only to ask one question: were you called and sent by Jesus Christ, the

Head of the church, under the direction of the Holy Spirit? You're an apostle if the Holy Spirit has sent you to a mission field. If you weren't sent by the Holy Spirit, even if you're doing commendable things, you're merely a nice person performing altruistic deeds. The qualifying word is *sent*. The same is true whether the ministry is big or small, whether in a church building or the marketplace; the question remains: Were you sent?

This can be seen in Acts 13:1, where two of the five prophets and teachers in the church at Antioch are chosen by the Holy Spirit and sent out. In Acts 13:4, Luke says, *"So, being sent out by the Holy Spirit, they went down to Seleucia"*. One chapter later, in Acts 14:14, Paul and Silas, previously called teachers or prophets, are now called apostles. What differentiates teachers and prophets from the office of an apostle? Apostles were sent, and they are on an assignment. Also noteworthy is that apostles were chosen among teachers and prophets, not pastors.

Our responsibility is to recognize those whom the Holy Spirit has sent (as noted in identifiers and releasers above).

Their responsibility is to say "Yes" to His call.

When Jesus called the original disciples (Matthew 10, Mark 3, Luke 6 and 9), He sent them. As soon as they were dispersed, their designation changed from disciples to apostles.

In Luke 10, Jesus sends out seventy-two disciples. Again, as soon as they are sent, their responsibilities change to that of an apostle. Jesus commissioned them to heal the sick and announce the kingdom of God.

When Jesus called the eleven in the upper room

following His resurrection, He sent them out with these words, *"As the Father has **sent** me, even so I am **sending** you"* (John 20:21, emphasis added).

In the gospel of John, Jesus often referred to the fact that the Father had sent Him. The word *sent, pempo* in Greek, is the root word for *apostle;* it is used forty-three times in John's gospel alone to refer to Jesus. This is confirmed in Hebrews 3:1: *"Therefore, holy brothers, you who share in a heavenly calling, consider Jesus, the **apostle** and high priest of our confession."*

Jesus, whom the Father sent, sent out the disciples. After His resurrection, the disciples, under the direction of the Holy Spirit, sent out disciples.

There were five men in Acts 13 called to be teachers and prophets, Barnabas, Simeon, who was called Niger; Lucius of Cyrene; Manaen, a friend of Herod; and Saul, later called the apostle Paul. What a great pool of leaders from which to draw. I'm convinced that there are apostles, prophets, evangelists, and teachers in every church if we don't get stuck on one office only, the pastor.

I know it's the practice of most church staff that when a position becomes available, they head straight for the roster of professionals. I suggest it might be more productive and healthier for the church if they begin to look at those sitting in front of them every Sunday. The New Testament church didn't grow through acquiring professionals but through training and releasing volunteers, many new believers. You are either a training/sending church, or you are borrowing your ministers from others who are. That's too bad.

How Do We Change from Pastoral-led Church Leadership to the Apostolic and Prophetic Foundation?

It's rather simple. Start with yourself. If you can find and identify your calling, it will open the door to other Spirit-led changes. If you were called to be an apostle and know you were sent, begin to move in your anointing. I'm not talking about tacking a sign on your office door or posting a reserved sign on your parking spot identifying you as an apostle. We don't need any more titles. Don't be enamored by them. All we are and all we will ever be is a servant. I will spend a chapter discussing this issue later.

While we can and should shy away from promoting ourselves through titles, we must understand our calling and function with confidence in it. Hopefully, *humility* will drive you to shun the title, but *sensitivity* to the Holy Spirit will lead you to embrace the call.

It is important that you don't call or send yourself. Jesus said that if He bore witness about Himself, it would make His calling invalid. *"If I alone bear witness about myself, my testimony is not true"* (John 5:31). The same is true of all of us. Only God and others can validate you.

Who Will Validate My Call?

If God has called you, He will use flesh and blood people to validate your calling. In Jesus' case, it was John the Baptist. For you, it will most likely be from people you haven't in some way influenced; it must be supernatural. And God forbid that your paid staff are the only ones validating your calling.

Regardless of the messenger, the Holy Spirit will always speak through a human vessel to confirm heaven's call on your life. This can happen anytime, whether as a small child or a mature adult. And the confirmation can be at multiple stages and with different people confirming your call. God continues to validate His will through the voice of "two or three witnesses."

The Laying On of Hands

It appears that the laying on of hands in the New Testament was more than a nice gesture and a religious symbol, but a prophetic action sanctioned by Paul, the writer of Hebrews, and the New Testament church, confirming publicly on earth what had already been commissioned in heaven. See Hebrews 6:2; 1 Timothy 4:14; 2 Timothy 1:6; Acts 13:3.

The Bible says, *"Do not be hasty in the laying on of hands"* (1 Timothy 5:22). The previous chapter shows the laying on of hands by the presbytery, which, when given prophetically, is powerful in its application. We might even consider this the time of ordination for those called. *"Do not neglect the gift you have, which was given you by prophecy when the council of elders laid their hands on you"* (1 Timothy 4:14).

Apostle-led versus Pastor-led Churches

You may still be asking what this looks like in my local church. It is essential to differentiate between pastoral and apostolic leadership within the local church and the subsequent impact on the world. As mentioned in the introduction, I once ascribed to the non-biblical view of building the church versus Christ's admonition to build the kingdom. I pastored with this myopic view, focusing only on my sheep, my church, and my activities. The following observations arise from that season and my subsequent correction to focus on the kingdom of God. These comparisons are by no means exhaustive, nor are they tendencies that are always in place, all the time. As a lighthouse signals danger ahead, these observations can warn us when we are off course from the biblical foundation of apostles and prophets.

Pastor-led Churches

1. Concentrate more on the physical building and those who attend.
2. Concentrate more on the program of the church rather than evangelism.
3. Spend most of the income on the local church building and in-house programs.
4. View the church as more important than the kingdom of God.
5. All authority rests in the pastor, with little or no attention, finances, or recognition given to the apostles, prophets, evangelists, and teachers. Accountability to apostles and prophets is absent, and their presence and activity are notably absent on a Sunday.
6. Most of the work is done by the pastoral staff and volunteers, but most of the congregation has little or no responsibility.
7. The church building itself is significant, even to the distortion of who the real church is, the people.
8. Concentrate on getting people into the building rather than sending people out. The church has

promoted a "Come" gospel rather than a "Go"
gospel.

9. Tend to be sectarian, protective, provincial, and
possessive of the members. The church members
"belong" to the pastors and no one else. People
are blessed when they come in and are cursed
when they leave, perpetuating a culture of fear.

10. Honor only the top leadership rather than
celebrating all the members.

11. Liberal donors receive undue and excessive
attention.

Apostle-led Churches

1. See the city / region, not the building, as the locus
and focus of ministry.

2. See themselves as a releaser of ministries.

3. Networks in the skeletal structure of the body of
Christ (Ephesians 4:16 and Colossians 2:19).

4. See the body of Christ in any area as one,
comprised of all born-again believers, not just
their particular ministry. Every ethnicity is not
only welcomed but celebrated.

5. Promote Jesus as the Head of the church, not a
pastor, prophet, or even apostle.

6. The church grows organically, not by program,
but by prayer.

7. All members do the work of the ministry, not just
a few.

8. Concentrate on the growth of the kingdom of God more than the local church.
9. Value diversity of gifts and callings.
10. Seek and promote unity in the body of Christ.
11. Identify and release gifted men and women.
12. Operate in the supernatural.
13. Bind the controlling powers of darkness in the area. The church in Ephesus, in Acts 19, is an excellent example.

In support of the final point, I want to quote one more time from Paul. *"The signs of a true apostle were performed among you with utmost patience, with signs and wonders and mighty works"* (2 Corinthians 12:12). The church needs foundational leaders to reach this world.

The Skeletal Structure of the Body

Paul gives several Scriptures that identify the church's offices as body parts, particularly as joints and ligaments. These offices function similarly to the ligaments and tendons in the body; they join the bones, or the muscles to the bone. In other words, they act as a buffer between the bones. This is an essential role that both the apostle and prophet fulfill in the church.

The two Greek words for *joints* and *ligaments* are *haphe* and *sundesmon*. Ephesians 4:15–16 puts it this way:

"Rather, speaking the truth in love, we are to grow up in every way into Him who is the head, into Christ, from whom the whole body, joined and held together by every joint [haphe] *with which it is equipped, when each part is working properly, makes the body grow so that it builds itself up in love."*

Colossians 2:19 says, *"…and not holding fast to the Head, from whom the whole body, nourished and knit together through its joints* [haphe] *and ligaments,* [syndesmon] *grows with a growth that is from God."*

Whether you translate the Greek words as joints, ligaments, tendons, or sinew, the meaning remains the same; they all connect tissue, bonding body parts together. What could be more descriptive of the offices and leaders of the church? Though at times we have unfortunately been more divisive than uniting, our true purpose is to bring connection to the diverse members of the body, allowing us all to grow up together into our Head, Jesus Christ. As Paul mentioned, this takes great patience.

Apostles and prophets are networkers, continually joining disparate body members together so the body can be united and grow into the headship of Jesus. A person must be a networker to qualify for the ascension gifts of apostles or prophets.

If we ignore, underuse, or disregard the most foundational leaders of the body, apostles, and prophets, we will sorely lack cohesion in the body of Christ. We will be like a body without a skeletal structure, unable to function. The gates of Hades will certainly not be demoralized and disarmed by our quivering presence.

Where Are the Prophets?

I can say, like Amos of old, *"I was no prophet, nor a prophet's son"* (Amos 7:14), but I can spot them when I see them.

Before addressing prophets, I want to clarify that I don't believe that the New Testament prophet is the same as the

Old Testament prophets who penned the canon of
Scripture. Jesus stated unequivocally that John the Baptist
was the end of the line for the Old Testament prophets. *"For
all the Prophets and the Law prophesied until John"* (Matthew
11:13). Hebrews states, *"Long ago, at many times and in many
ways, God spoke to our fathers by the prophets, but in these last
days he has spoken to us by his Son, whom he appointed the heir
of all things, through whom also he created the world"* (Hebrews
1:1–2).

God is no longer speaking infallible words to prophets
moved on by the Holy Spirit to lay down the canon of
Scripture, as He did during the composing of the Old
Testament. That doesn't mean, however, that God is no
longer speaking to men and women the same as He has
always done. God spoke through many prophets in both
Testaments who would not ultimately become authors of
Scripture.

- God told Abimelech that Abraham was a
  prophet, though he never penned what would
  become the canon of Scripture. *"Now then, return
  the man's wife, for he is a prophet, so that he will pray
  for you and you shall live"* (Genesis 20:7). As an
  aside, this is the very first mention of the word
  prophet in Scripture.
- In Exodus 7, Aaron, the brother of Moses, is
  called a prophet, though he never penned any of
  the books of the Old Testament.
- In Numbers, YHWH committed to speaking to
  prophets, who were non-biblical writers, in either

dreams or visions. *"And he said, 'Hear my words: If there is a prophet among you, I the LORD make myself known to him in a vision; I speak with him in a dream'"* (Numbers 12:6).

- I love the ministry of the non-writing leadership prophets who prophesied in the camp in Numbers 11 after receiving the spirit of Moses. When Joshua remonstrated that Eldad and Medad continued to prophesy in the camp, Moses responded, *"Are you jealous for my sake? Would **that all the LORD'S people were prophets**, that the LORD would put his spirit on them"* (Number 11:29, emphasis added).

The New Testament Office of Prophet versus Prophecy

In his letter to the Corinthians, Paul appears to echo the words of Moses. *"Now I want you all to speak in tongues, but even more to prophesy. The one who prophesies is greater than the one who speaks in tongues, unless someone interprets, so that the church may be built up"* (1 Corinthians 14:5). Therein lies the heart of prophecy. It is for the edification and building up of the body of Christ.

But is there a distinction between the office of prophet and prophecy? Biblically, yes. The office of the prophet is distinguished in much the same way as the office of the apostle. These individuals will be identified and released by the community in which they abide. I believe God speaks to men and women today who are called to faithfully convey God's message to the church. As much as we need the gift of apostles, we also need the gift of prophets. First, let's examine the role of the prophet.

The Role of the Prophet

When a man or woman hears from God, they must accurately convey that message to the church, individually or corporately. God has spoken since Genesis 1:3 and John 1:1 and continues to speak to this day. God always has a mouthpiece, and that mouthpiece is called a prophet.

When Jesus spoke of the Holy Spirit, He said,

"When the Spirit of truth comes, he will guide you into all the truth, for he will not speak on his own authority, but whatever he hears he will speak, and he will declare to you the things that are to come. He will glorify me, for he will take what is mine and declare it to you. All that the Father has is mine; therefore I said that he will take what is mine and declare it to you" (John 16:13–15).

Part of the Holy Spirit's church-age responsibility is to reveal what will come. That is called revelation, God's "now" voice to you. Those who think God stopped speaking when John wrote, *"Amen. Come, Lord Jesus"* (Revelation 22:20), have not considered the entirety of God's Word. Though the canon of Scripture is set and will never be added to or subtracted from, God continues to speak, but it will never contradict the Word of God. If it does, it's not God.

Notice how much the Lord wants to speak to people through the prophets. According to the New Testament, *"the testimony* [Greek: *marturia*] *of Jesus is the spirit of prophecy"* (Revelation 19:10). From this word, we get the word *martyr*. The two martyred witnesses in Revelation are called prophets. In fact, we are told that the people in heaven overcame the accuser *"by the blood of the Lamb and by the word of their testimony, and they did not love their lives to the death"* (Revelation 12:11 NKJV). We cannot have the witness of Jesus without the spirit of prophecy.

Prophets are also one of the categories of people to be rewarded in God's new kingdom. *"The nations raged, but your wrath came, and the time for the dead to be judged, and for rewarding your servants, the prophets and saints, and those who fear your name, both small and great"* (Revelation 11:18).

As noted, some New Testament prophets mentioned by name are Silas, Judas, and Agabus. At least some men mentioned in Acts 13 are singled out as prophets, though none contributed to the writing of any of the New Testament, except Saul of Tarsus (Paul). These were men and women, including Philip's daughters, who clearly heard from the Lord and conveyed His message to the church.

I'm unconvinced that the primary responsibility of the New Testament prophet is to give people direction. Though I recognize it could include direction, such as Agabus's prophecy to Paul in Acts 21, I don't believe that giving people direction is the major purpose of the New Testament prophet or prophecy. That is the responsibility of the Holy Spirit. Paul states the purpose of prophecy is to "edify, encourage and comfort" (1 Corinthians 14:3). I believe that any prophetic word should be confirmation versus information. Remember, despite Agabus's accurate warning to Paul that he would face great adversity if he went to Rome, Paul did not allow it to sway him. He knew that as he had given testimony to Jesus in Jerusalem, regardless of the cost, he must do the same in Rome (Acts 23:11).

God Still Speaks to His Church

I also do not believe the cessationism view that the charismatic gifts and the ascension offices of the church ceased with the completion of John's Revelation, ca. AD 96. If Paul penned the words in 1 Corinthians 13 from Ephesus, sometime between AD 53–55, it is strange to me that they would no longer be valid in less than fifty years.

Neither do I believe that which is "perfect," in 1 Corinthians 13:10, refers to the Word of God. The Word has existed for nearly 1,400 years and doesn't "become" perfect. It refers to Jesus Himself at His second advent, when we see Him *"face to face"* (1 Corinthians 13:12). Jesus is the only "perfect man" in Scripture. He was the only man born perfect and who attained perfection through earthly life. Jesus was born perfect (*teleios* in Greek) at His birth and became perfect/ *teleios* through His obedience (Hebrews 5:8–9).

Besides, knowledge, tongues, and prophecy will all cease simultaneously in this Scripture. If tongues and prophecy cease with knowledge, this approach undermines your intellectual ability to interpret properly. If we lost tongues and prophecy at the conclusion of the New Testament canon, we also lost knowledge, not a pleasant thought.

I am convinced that God still speaks to people today, and more so as the day approaches for Jesus' return. As you read in the Scriptures quoted above, Revelation references the prophetic and prophets, and the testimony (witness) of Jesus is the spirit of prophecy (Revelation 19:10).

Down through the ages, God has spoken to people through people. Sometimes, it's a still, small voice, and at other times, it thunders. When the Scripture says, *"And the Holy Spirit said,"* as in Acts 13:2, He most likely used the mouth of a human instrument.

Prophecy versus Prophet

So, what, then, is the differentiator between the office of the prophet and prophecy? 1 Corinthians 12:7–11 describes the manifest gifts of the Holy Spirit, where prophecy is listed as an activity of the Holy Spirit given as needed through the believer for the edification of the body of Christ in the moment. You needn't be a prophet to experience this gift. As you posture yourself to be available to the Spirit's work, you can participate in His activity everywhere you go. Remember, the offices and gifts of the Spirit are designed to work in tandem with one another. Think of it this way…

The Balance of Pomegranates and Bells

In the Old Testament, the borders of the robes of the high priest were ringed alternately with pomegranates and bells. In the same way, the Holy Spirit has chosen that the offices, gifts, and fruit of the Spirit be arranged alternately to complement each other.

In 1 Corinthians, the gifts of the Spirit are placed strategically between the five offices of the Spirit and the administrative gifts. *"And God has appointed in the church first apostles, second prophets, third teachers, then miracles, then gifts*

of healing, helping, administrating and various kinds of tongues"
(1 Corinthians 12:28).

John 14–16 records Jesus' introduction of the coming
paraclete, or helper, the Holy Spirit. Chapters 14 and 16
reveal the person and purpose of the Holy Spirit, while
chapter 15 introduces Jesus, neatly sandwiched between the
two, as the True Vine. Pomegranates and bells are
everywhere. Balance is the principle of God.

The church has operated so long with just
pomegranates (the fruit of the Spirit) that it has no idea
who or what the bells (the gifts and the offices of the
Spirit) are. We must balance the apostolic and prophetic
ascension gifts and the charismatic gifts and fruit of the
Spirit to be a balanced kingdom of priests without
discounting either. Therefore, we do not discount the office
of the prophet or the believer operating in the prophetic in
the moment.

The Holy Spirit's Presence upon the Believer

People began to prophesy in the Old and New
Testaments when the Holy Spirit came upon them. There is
no mention that they held the office of prophet.

- When the Spirit came upon the seventy elders,
  they began to prophesy (Numbers 11:25).
- When the Spirit came upon Saul, he began to
  prophesy (1 Samuel 10:10; 19:18–24).
- When the Spirit of the Lord came upon
  Zechariah, he prophesied (Luke 1:67).
- The Ephesian believers began to prophesy when
  the Spirit came upon them (Acts 19:6).

The Word predicts that the Holy Spirit will come upon our sons and daughters in the last days, and they will prophesy (Joel 2:28 and Acts 2:17).

In Revelation 10:11, the angel instructed John the Beloved, one of the original disciples, to *"prophesy about many peoples and nations and languages and kings."*

1 Peter 4:11 fits into the prophetic category. *"whoever speaks, as one who speaks oracles of God"*. The Greek word for *oracles* is *logion,* meaning one who speaks words or gives utterances from God. *Logion* is mentioned only four times in the New Testament and clearly means an utterance from God. I hope that the preaching of God's servants includes words that come straight from the heart of God and penetrate deep into the soul, both convicting and liberating. I know I've experienced the divine when I spoke words that I knew were not mine but found their origin in heaven. It was not part of written or memorized notes but the Holy Spirit moving through me to touch the hearts of the hearers.

I've also been on the opposite side of the pulpit when, from the pew, I could sense the moment the speaker's words turned from human origin to divine, when their scripted comments turned into spontaneous Holy Spirit dictum, with Spirit-convicting, convincing power, pure prophecy.

When my mother, Rachel Titus, spoke, she would often interrupt her message with words of knowledge to people in the congregation. The words were so specific that people knew they were from God. Once, she said, "There is a man in the congregation who buried your tithes in a tin can in the backyard. The Lord wants you to know He knows they are there," then continued preaching. Following the service, a furious man attacked the pastor.

"Don't blame me," the pastor responded. "I didn't know that. You better dig up your tin can. It appears God wants His money."

On another occasion in Mena, Arkansas, my mother spoke piercing words from the pulpit. "There is a man here today who will not be given another chance. God has spoken multiple times in the past, and you have rejected His invitation. Today will be your last opportunity to receive His Son."

The next day, we heard the ambulance drive by our motel. The man she had spoken to was out mowing his lawn when he dropped dead of a heart attack. We only pray he heeded the words.

My mother was forthright; she did not embellish what she heard, but her words were always driven by love.

Love, Wisdom, and Prophecy

In 1 Corinthians 13:2–3 Paul says, "*And if I have prophetic powers, and understand all mysteries and all knowledge…but do not have love, I gain nothing.*" That's a lot of prophetic anointing, but without love, you gain nothing. Anytime the Holy Spirit moves upon you to give a prophetic word, it will be bathed in love, and there will be no self in it.

Again, Paul admonished that "*the person who prophesies speaks to people for their strengthening, encouraging and comfort*" (1 Corinthians 14:3). Do you know how many people need a prophetically inspired encouraging word? Years ago, I thought I had the "gift of criticism" (found nowhere in the Bible, incidentally) until the Lord got a hold of me and changed my heart. Since then, I have determined that my words will align with the prophetic spirit of God by encouraging the body of Christ.

It is also vital to remember that prophecy is listed alongside wisdom in 1 Corinthians 12. I often sense a word God has for someone, but in tandem with wisdom, I have chosen to be silent, sensing that the time is not right. Ultimately, it is essential to remember that if God wants His children to hear something badly enough, He can get the message across even if it doesn't come through you. Pride has no place in the prophetic. In the same work mentioned above, J. Rodman Williams states: "True prophecy is thoroughly grounded in Scripture and based upon it, speaks forth God's particular word for the contemporary scene."

A House on the Rock

Jesus' teaching is clear. He warns that the house built on sand will not stand, but the house on the rock will endure every storm hurled against it and not fall (Matthew 7:24–27). Jesus is our firm foundation. As the Head of the church, He has told us how to build. If we continue to build upon the sand, dismissing His words, our house will crumble. This is precisely what we are witnessing in the church today.

But it is not too late! I firmly believe that in the last days, God will raise authentic, Spirit-led, Spirit-anointed apostles and prophets who will restore the church to its original foundation.

CHAPTER 2
PREACH THE KINGDOM OF GOD

"And proclaim as you go, saying, 'The kingdom of heaven is at hand'" (Matthew 10:7).

"And this gospel of the kingdom will be proclaimed throughout the whole world as a testimony to all nations, and then the end will come" (Matthew 24:14).

When the elders of Israel demanded a king they could see instead of the God they could not, the Lord reassured His aging prophet, Samuel, *"Obey the voice of the people in all that they say to you, for they have not rejected you, but they have rejected me from being king over them"* (1 Samuel 8:1). Samuel warned the elders that an earthly king would ultimately enslave them to his whims. Nonetheless, the elders persisted, and Samuel anointed Saul as king. Thus began a reign of kings ending in complete and utter turmoil—as predicted.

Woven through the subsequent history of kings and

kingdoms in the Old Testament is a powerful key essential
to understanding the importance of the kingdom of God.

As the King Went, So Did His People

If the king followed God and feared Him, battles were
won, idol worship was mostly demolished, people and lands
prospered, and peace ensued. The fruit of godless kings is
quite the opposite—destruction in battle, a people enslaved
and scattered, and rampant idolatry. When the people
rejected God as king, they were left vulnerable to the enemy
and exiled to foreign lands. During this period, the prophets
began to speak of a messiah. *"For thus says the LORD of hosts:
'He sent Me after glory, to the nations which plunder you; for he
who touches you touches the apple of His eye'"* (Zechariah 2:8
NKJV). Essentially, the "apple of the eye" refers to the pupil,
or the center of our eyes, and the most sensitive part. This
means that any affront to the people of God is an affront to
God, who personalizes the pain of His people. A literal poke
in His eye. Because of this, He promised, *"Many nations shall
be joined to the LORD in that day, and they shall become My
people. And I will dwell in your midst"* (Zechariah 2:11 NKJV).

God's Kingdom Come

Five hundred years after this prophecy, the promised
messiah, Jesus, emerged from the wilderness *full of power*
(Luke 4:14), declaring the kingdom (*basileia* meaning *reign*)
of God, and dwelt in our midst. The invisible God made
visible in the person of Jesus (Colossians 1:5–29) brought
His invisible kingdom. As it was for the people of old, the
king determined the people's prosperity. Under Christ's
rule, God's people were assured:

- Victory in the battle over Satan and the kingdoms of darkness;
- The restoration of true worship in relationship to God;
- Freedom to prosper under the Prince of Peace;
- Powerful keys and spiritual gifts to equip and edify Christ's body.

With so much at stake, why have we stopped preaching the kingdom of God, the very thing Jesus commanded us to do? (Matthew 24:14) And if we are not preaching the kingdom of God from our pulpits, what are we preaching?

The "Gospel of the Church" versus the "Gospel of the Kingdom."

As I said in the introduction, it seems logical that if the church understood the power of kingdom keys, it would devastate the kingdoms of darkness, put the enemy under its feet, and establish the kingdom of God. Yet we continue trying to build the church, which Jesus said was **His** possession that **He** would build, and neglect building the kingdom of God, which is **our** responsibility to build. We've constructed a new gospel that advances the church rather than the kingdom.

So impactful was the kingdom's impact and so benevolent the loving Savior King, the early church endured unbelievable persecution to advance its gospel. In due course, Emperor Constantine declared Christianity the religion of Rome. Persecuted Christians found freedom to worship safely and, commissioned by the emperor, began to build churches. Soon, the gospel of the kingdom was replaced by the "gospel of the church," and its disciples have been consumed with it for the past two thousand years.

This "gospel" christened the building as the church rather than the *ekklesia,* the people, and coronated the pastor as king. The church and its program replaced the message of Jesus and His kingdom. The gospel changed from a "go" gospel to a "come" gospel. We tell people to come and hear a preacher. Come, listen to good worship music. Come to the children's program, come to an evangelistic crusade.

The warning of Stephen before being stoned to death is forgotten: *"the Most High does not dwell in houses made by hands"* (Acts 7:48).

The Church in Their House

The idea that the church is a building for people to come to is so entrenched in the average believer that changing modern nomenclature to biblical language is nearly impossible. On Sunday morning, we say, "Let's go to church." What if we were to say: "The **church** is driving to the building. Following a time of worship, fellowship, and a lesson in the Word, the **church** will return to the car and drive back to their home." People would think we're crazy. Yet this is not only accurate, it's biblical.

Paul put it this way, *"Greet also the church in their* [Prisca and Aquila's] *house"* (Romans 16:5). The building was merely a place for the *ekklesia,* the church, to meet.

The church's most common name in the New Testament is the body of Christ. Therefore, let's consider the church as a body and not a building, a body built through relationships with Jesus and others, not physically erected on stone foundations. This will help us discover the church's true purpose, Jesus' body reaching out to the world rather than a building to visit on Sundays.

I like to consider the church covering a locality of people from all denominations and independent groups. If Jesus Christ is your Lord and Savior, you are part of the same body, His church, regardless of what building you meet in. One pastor told me, "I've had many people leave our church and go to your church."

"That's impossible," I responded. "I don't have a church, and you don't either. Only Jesus has a church. That means people can change buildings, or miss attending a few Sundays, and still be a member of the only church in the city, Jesus' church."

The Bride of Christ

The church constantly references the "bride of Christ," a term used four times in the New Testament and not until Revelation 19. If you're familiar with Revelation 19, you know that the chapter refers to Jesus at His second coming, which most Christians agree has not yet happened. We must clearly understand that until Jesus returns, the church is His betrothed body. All that changes at the marriage supper of the Lamb, an event yet to occur, when the bride of Christ is introduced.

Why is this distinction important? When God created Adam, Eve was inside of Adam. It was only after Adam was put to sleep that Eve was created from his side (Genesis 2:22). The moment the resurrected church, the body of Christ, becomes the bride, it will be at the marriage supper of the Lamb. *"Hallelujah! For the Lord our God the Almighty reigns. Let us rejoice and exult and give the glory, for the marriage of the Lamb has come, and his Bride has made herself ready"* (Revelation 19:6–7). In *The Book of Revelation: The New International Commentary of the New Testament,* Mounce states:

In biblical times a marriage involved two major events, the betrothal and the wedding. These were normally separated by a period of time during which the two individuals were considered husband and wife and as such were under the obligations of faithfulness.

Before the marriage of the Lamb takes place, we are His betrothed body, operating under His headship (Ephesians 5:22–24). As His betrothed, we live to please Him. We move where and when He desires to exercise His authority faithfully. Until the marriage, much work must be done to advance His kingdom. If we see ourselves in the fulfillment of marriage rather than the preparation of marriage, we risk falling asleep, as did five of the ten virgins (Matthew 25).

Numerous references in the New Testament call the Church the body of Christ. *"And he put all things under his feet and gave him as head over all things to the church, which is his body, the fullness of him who fills all in all"* (Ephesians 1:22–23) and *"And he is the head of the body, the church"* (Colossians 1:18), to name a few.

This is critical to our understanding of how we operate in His authority and power on this earth. If the kingdom of the world, the powers of hell, demons, serpents, scorpions, and even the devil himself are to be put under the feet of Jesus, it would be good to identify who His feet are. Jesus is the head in heaven, and His body is on earth, carrying out

His purpose. The feet and hands are attached to the body, thus Jesus' representation on this earth. We are the operational part of Jesus' body until the day we stand at His side. Unless we know exactly who we are, we will never know how to fulfill His will.

Your Kingdom Come

These are the words of the prayer Jesus taught His disciples to pray in Matthew 6:10. The kingdom of God is central to all of Jesus' teachings and a major theme throughout the Bible.

The longest and most definitive kingdom in the Old Testament is found in Daniel 7. During the final year of Belshazzar, king of Babylon, ca. 553 BC, Daniel had a dream of four great world empires and their destruction at the hands of the Ancient of Days, God the Father, and the Son of Man.

At the conclusion of world history, these great empires, which are still in existence today, will be stripped of their power, and their kingdoms will be given to the saints of the Most High.

- We know who the kingdoms are: Babylon, current Iraq, Persia, current Iran, Greece, and Rome.
- We know who the Ancient of Days is, and He is also called the Most High God (*El Elyon*), known to us in the New Testament as the Father of our Lord Jesus Christ.
- We also know who the Son of Man is. In the New

Testament, Jesus calls Himself the Son of Man over eighty times.

- The saints of the Most High God are those who believe in the Lord Jesus Christ and have been made holy by His blood.

Also mentioned in his vision are four beasts. Out of the fourth beast comes a ruler, known in the New Testament as the Antichrist, the Beast, who wars against the saints. In the days of this evil ruler, the Ancient of Days shall destroy his kingdom and give it to His Son, and the saints will possess the kingdom forever.

Earlier in the book of Daniel, the four kingdoms mentioned above are destroyed. *"And in the days of these kings the God of heaven will set up a kingdom which shall never be destroyed"* (Daniel 2:44). A stone not hewn with hands, a reference to the Son of Man, rolls down from the mountain from which it is hewn, striking and destroying the statue that represents the kingdoms of the world and crushing them to powder.

The Dominion of the Kingdom of God

The message is clear. All nations, civilizations, rulers, dominions, and world powers will eventually bow before the Lord Jesus Christ. *"at the name of Jesus every knee should bow, in heaven and on earth and under the earth, and every tongue confess that Jesus Christ is Lord, to the glory of God the Father"* (Philippians 2:10–11).

The book of Revelation also captures this event: *"Then the seventh angel blew his trumpet, and there were loud voices in heaven, saying, 'The kingdom of the world has become the kingdom of our Lord and of his Christ, and he shall reign forever and ever'"* (Revelation 11:15). Not only is the proclamation made, but it is made loudly.

Revelation 19 reveals what will happen when Jesus returns:

"And the armies of the heaven, arrayed in fine linen, white and pure, were following him on white horses. From his mouth comes a sharp sword with which to strike down the nations, and he will rule them with a rod of iron… On his robe and on his thigh, he has a name written, 'King of kings and Lord of lords'" (Revelation 19:14–16).

The prophecies of Daniel and John in the book of Revelation are the two bookends of the kingdom in human history. They reveal both the beginning of Satan's kingdom, reaching back to Babylon, and the Tower of Babel.. The major teaching on the kingdom, the filling of the eschatological sandwich, would have to wait until Jesus arrived on the scene, as recorded in the Gospels.

The Gospel and the Kingdom

I am amazed at how the church has focused on "the church," its spending, message, and program while spending so little time focusing on the main topic in the Bible, the kingdom of God. It is the *complete opposite* of what Jesus, the founder and Head of the church, did.

Jesus mentioned the church in only two places, Matthew 16:18 and Matthew 18:17, yet He spoke on the kingdom of God (or of heaven, as Matthew generally states it) over one hundred times in the Gospels.

- It was His first and last sermon (Mathew 4:17; Acts 1:3).
- He preached on the kingdom in every town and village of Galilee (Matthew 4:23; 9:35).
- He sent out the twelve disciples to proclaim the kingdom of God (Matthew 10:7).
- He sent out seventy-two (some manuscripts say seventy) to preach on the kingdom of God (Luke 10:9).
- As commissioned by Jesus, the early church preached on the kingdom of God (Acts 8:12).
- He sent Paul to Rome to preach on the kingdom of God (Acts 28:28–30).
- The majority of His parables were on the kingdom of God (Matthew 13:11–52 specifically verses 11, 19, 24, 31, 33, 38, 41, 43, 44, 45, and 52. Also, Matthew chapters 19, 20, 21, 22, 24, 25).
- Jesus gave the church the keys to the kingdom of God (Matthew 16:19).
- Jesus taught the disciples to pray daily for the kingdom of God to come (Matthew 6:10).
- Jesus said to *"seek first the kingdom of God and His righteousness"* (Matthew 6:33).
- Jesus said you must be *"born again"* to enter the kingdom of God (John 3:3–5).
- The kingdom of God comes upon people when Jesus casts out demons by the Holy Spirit (Matthew 12:28; Luke 11:20).
- The message of the kingdom includes healing the

sick, raising the dead, cleansing lepers, and casting out demons (Matthew 10:7–8).

- The end will come when the gospel of the kingdom is preached throughout the world (Matthew 24:14).
- The church, the body of Christ, will be the instrument to destroy the kingdom of the world (1 Corinthians 15:22–25).
- Flesh and blood cannot inherit the kingdom of God (1 Corinthians 15:50).

And it's not as if the Gospels are the only place in the New Testament where the kingdom is taught. These are a few additional New Testament references:

Acts 1:3, 6; 8:12; 14:22; 19:8; 20:25; 28:23, 31

Romans 14:17

1 Corinthians 4:20; 6:9–10; 15:24–28; 15:50

Galatians 5:21

Ephesians 5:5

Colossians 1:13; 4:11

1 Thessalonians 2:12

2 Thessalonians 1:5

2 Timothy 4:1

2 Timothy 4:18

Hebrews 1:8; 12:28

James 2:5

2 Peter 1:11

Revelation 11:15

The Invisible Kingdom

I have a rather simplistic definition of the kingdom juxtaposed with the church.

The church represents *who* we are.
The kingdom represents *our activity.*

But if the church is viewed as a building instead of as the body of Christ:

The church operates on Sundays.
The kingdom operates daily.

The church attempts to get people inside the building.
The kingdom tries to get people out of the building.

The church wants to fill the pews.
The kingdom seeks to destroy the devil's works.

Perhaps the invisible nature of the kingdom of God causes people to reduce it to a church building. It's an honest mistake; the building is a tangible place to visit. Let's not forget that the Israelites rejected the invisible God in favor of a visible earthly king. Let's also not forget that when the kingdom of God is advanced, the invisible forces of darkness are exposed visibly. People are visibly healed and delivered. That is a far more powerful way to operate than as a building that shuts its doors when the service is over.

The Conquest of King Jesus

When Jesus announced His kingdom, it was not just

47

within the context of Roman rule. Ever present and in full operation was the kingdom of darkness, another invisible kingdom manifesting visibly in all sorts of vile corruption and evil.

During Christ's temptation in the wilderness (Matthew 4, Mark 1, and Luke 4), the devil took Jesus up to a high mountain and showed Him all the world's kingdoms. In any high mountain in the Judean hills above Jerusalem, it would be easy to look east toward Babylon and Persia and west toward Greece and Rome.

After the panoramic display of the world's civilizations, the devil made Jesus an offer:

"All these I will give you, if you will fall down and worship me" (Matthew 4:9). The story is riddled with truth and error. It was true that the world's kingdoms were under the devil's authority and still are to this day. 2 Corinthians 4:4 says that the devil is the god of this world. In John's gospel, 12:31, 14:30, and 16:11, Jesus called the devil the ruler of this world. 1 John 5:19 says the whole world is under the power of the evil one. Ephesians 2:2 identifies Satan as the prince of the authorities of the air, and Revelation 9 depicts him as the king of the Abyss. These Scriptures, and more, sound convincing that the devil and not God is the ruler of this world.

It doesn't take much discernment to know that the media, education, communications, economy, music, and world governments are all in the firm control of the devil. Sound travels through air, and he is the *"prince of the power of the air"* (Ephesians 2:2). When man sinned in the garden of Eden, he lost His title right to rule the world; death and sin entered in, and the devil took over. It's as simple and devastating as that.

Jesus was not deluded into thinking that if He would bow to the devil, all the world's kingdoms would be turned over to Him. Jesus knew that what we worship, we serve. He rebuked the devil with these words: *"You shall worship the Lord your God and him only shall you serve"* (Matthew 4:10). Jesus had another plan. He would go to the cross and destroy Death *and* the Destroyer.

One of my favorite Scriptures detailing this conquest is recorded in Colossians 2:15: *"He disarmed the rulers and authorities and put them to open shame, by triumphing over them in him."*

The devil's final conquest begins in Revelation 19. The Beast, also known as the Antichrist, and the False Prophet are thrown into the lake of fire. With two-thirds of the unholy trinity judged, the only one that remains is the devil himself. In Revelation 20, the devil himself, the founding father of the unholy trinity, is thrown into the bottomless pit for a thousand years. When the thousand years end, Satan is released for a time only to be forever thrown into a lake of fire with the Beast and False Prophet: *"and they will be tormented day and night forever and ever"* (Revelation 20:10).

The Purpose of Christ's Coming

The church is set between the cross and the return of Christ in power, biblically known as the Age of the Gentiles. During this time, the body of Christ has been called to finish what Christ started. Two Scriptures give a concise definition of the purpose of Christ's coming into the world:

"God anointed Jesus of Nazareth with the Holy Spirit and

with power. He went about doing good and healing all who were oppressed by the devil, for God was with him" (Acts 10:38).

"The reason the Son of God appeared was to destroy the works of the devil" (1 John 3:8).

If the purpose of Christ's coming was to destroy the works of the devil and his kingdom, that becomes, de facto, the responsibility of the church. Fortunately, in Luke 10:19, Jesus made it very clear that His body, the church, had the authority and power to accomplish the task.

The Domain of Darkness

Paul describes Satan's kingdom as the dominion or authority (Greek: *exousia*) of darkness. *"He has delivered us from the domain of darkness and transferred us to the kingdom of his beloved Son"* (Colossians 1:13).

Let's be clear: there are only two kingdoms. One is light, and the other is dark. Everyone is in one kingdom or another, and you are born into both. When you were born, you were born into a kingdom ruled over by Satan (Ephesians 2:1–3). When you are born again as a believer in Christ, you are transferred into a new kingdom, the kingdom of God (John 3:3,5). Authorities have changed. Both are eternal, but one reigns eternally as the King of Kings and Lord of Lords, and the other loses all authority and power and is eternally doomed to destruction.

In this present age, the church has authority over all the enemy's powers. The question is, are we exercising that authority?

John 3:19 says, *"And this is the judgment; the light has come into the world, and people loved the darkness rather than the light because their works were evil."* That tells it all. Darkness hates the light, and Jesus is light. That's great news for those who choose to walk in the light and bad news for those who prefer darkness. But it does not matter how dark the darkness is; you cannot extinguish the light. Darkness, as John 1:4 succinctly says, cannot overcome, overpower, or extinguish the light.

Challenging the Powers of Darkness

True kingdom revival will always challenge the powers of darkness. Demons, though the privates in Satan's army, are still part of the devil's hierarchy. When they are bound and cast out by the "stronger man" (Mark 3:27), the ripples go to the heavens, Satan's throne. Note that Satan is not permanently cast out of heaven until Revelation 12:10. Again, in Ephesians 2:2, he is called the prince of the authorities of the air.

Amazingly, nearly one-third of Jesus' miracles are related to delivering the demon-possessed. When the kingdom's King arrived, demons began demonstrating, and Jesus continually told them to be quiet. When I look for signs of revival in any given locality, I first look for demons demonstrating. While this might be an unsettling occurrence in a traditional church, it should be encouraging in a Spirit-filled church, where demons cannot exist in the presence and power of God and are forced to reveal themselves.

When the disciples returned from casting out demons, in Luke 10, Jesus said He saw *"Satan falling like lightning from heaven"* (Luke 10:18). This proves beyond doubt that the power of Jesus's name reaches to the heavens and paralyzes the powers of the devil. When the "strong man" is usurped by the stronger man, Satan's kingdom cannot stand.

Who Will Crush the Head of Satan?

The first prophecy in the Bible is found in Genesis 3:15, known to theologians as the *protoevangelium*. God tells the serpent, "*I will put enmity between you and the woman, and between your offspring and her offspring; he shall bruise your head and you shall bruise his heel.*"

The Hebrew word for *bruise* is *shuwph*, pronounced "shoof." It means to bruise, crush, seize, or strike at. The analogy is that of a stepped-upon snake. The snake will attempt to bite your heel, but you will crush its head. A snake bite to the foot can be painful and sometimes deadly to a man or woman, but stepping on the head of the snake is always fatal for the serpent.

Paul uses the same analogy in Romans 16:20 NLT: "*The God of peace will soon crush Satan under your feet.*" This verse, written decades after Jesus' death and resurrection, proves that the church, the body of Christ, is the agent God will use to crush Satan.

It is curious to me that the prophecy of Genesis 3:15 says the seed of the woman will "bruise" the head of the serpent, but Romans 16:20 declares that the church will "crush" the head of Satan. Jesus started the "bruising process," and the church will continue it until Satan's head is crushed.

God's Complete Authority

There could be no more complete commentary on authority than 1 Corinthians 15:24–28 NLT:

After that the end will come, when he [Jesus] will turn the kingdom over to God the Father, having destroyed every ruler and authority and power. For Christ must reign until he humbles all his enemies beneath his feet. And the last enemy to be destroyed is death. For the scriptures say, "God has put all things under his authority." (Of course, when it says "all things are under his authority," that does not include God himself, who gave Christ his authority.) Then, when all things are under his authority, the Son will put himself under God's authority, so that God, who gave His Son authority over all things, will be utterly supreme over everything everywhere.

You need to read these verses multiple times until they sink into your spirit. This is the singular mission of God since the fall of man: to reinstate His kingdom and authority through Jesus' life, death on the cross, and resurrection, and restore humankind to Himself.

Although Satan was paralyzed at the cross, he was allowed to continue his devilish authority over the realm of darkness until the return of Christ. And as you know, death, the last enemy to be destroyed, has not yet been put under the feet of Jesus. This will happen at the very end of Satan's reign (see 1 Corinthians 15:26, quoted above).

As I see it, if the world's kingdoms are to be put under Jesus' feet, the body of Christ must be the agent to bring that to pass. It's the body, the church, not the head, Jesus, that will crush the head of the serpent and destroy his kingdom. We are waiting for Jesus to destroy the works of the devil and usher in the kingdom, and Jesus is waiting for us to do it.

To ensure we understand, Paul said the end will come when every rule, authority, and power is put under His feet. It's clear to me that the feet of Jesus refer to the church, and the church is *the* agent to destroy the kingdoms of Satan and usher in the kingdom of God.

The Church's Complete Authority in Christ

I fear the church believes its primary purpose on earth is to prepare for heaven. Precious few have understood that the purpose of God for the church is the same as it was for Jesus, which is to destroy the works of the devil and put his kingdom under its feet. *"The Son of God came to destroy the works of the devil"* (1 John 3:8b NLT).

In Luke 10:17–19 NLT, when the disciples returned, claiming victory over demons, Jesus responded, *"I saw Satan fall from heaven like lightning."* Jesus said, *"Behold, I have given you authority to tread on serpents and scorpions, and over all the power of the enemy, and nothing shall hurt you"*

I'm not sure the church realizes the power and authority that Jesus entrusted it with. According to Matthew 16:19, Jesus says, *"I will give you the keys of the kingdom of heaven, and whatever you bind on earth shall be bound in heaven, and whatever you loose on earth shall be loosed in heaven."* The binding (forbidding) and loosing (allowing) nature of the keys is repeated in Revelation 20, where one angel, with the key to the bottomless pit (also called the Abyss), binds Satan for a thousand years. That is incredible authority. If one angel with one key can do that, what can the two-billion-member church do with the authority of Jesus and the keys to the kingdom of God? I'm not sure we fully comprehend the power and authority invested in us through the kingdom keys.

Through these past pages of kingdom teaching, I hope you've gained insight into the kingdom of God and its biblical importance for us today. The church's calling is more than building a big building where many people can visit. Our calling is to destroy the devil's works and claim his territory for Jesus. If our strategy isn't kingdom based, it's not biblical. We need to begin praying daily...

"Your kingdom come and your will be done on earth as it is in heaven" (Matthew 6:10).

CHAPTER 3
MAKE DISCIPLES OF ALL NATIONS

*"And he called to him his twelve disciples and he gave them
authority over unclean spirits, to cast them out, and to heal every
disease and every affliction"* (Matthew 10:1).

*"Go therefore and make disciples of all nations, baptizing
them in the name of the Father and of the Son and of the Holy
Spirit, teaching them to observe all that I have commanded you.
And behold, I am with you always, to the end of the age"*
(Matthew 28:19–20).

My friends created a simple discipleship reminder for
their daughter. Rather than telling her what not to do,
they stated their family values. "Our family is kind; our
family is respectful." There was a whole lot more they
wanted to say (and sometimes did), such as, "Don't do
that!" but they mainly chose to frame their values
positively.

If they helped someone in need, they would say, "Our
family is kind." If they witnessed impolite behavior, they

repeated the phrase. It wasn't overused. It was just used at key moments.

During her high school years, they noticed a positive difference in their daughter. Her friend group began to grow, as did her influence. On back-to-school night, they were approached by several parents with a similar testimony:

"Your daughter saved my daughter's life."

"My child was friendless, and when your daughter saw she was excluded, she befriended her."

When she got home, my friend asked her daughter to tell her about it. Her daughter replied, "You showed me that kindness changes lives, and I believed you."

Shaped for Destiny

I've heard it said that more is caught than taught. Discipleship is as much about what the disciple sees you doing as what they hear you saying. My friend's child witnessed her parents' kindness to others more than she heard them talk about it, and it shaped her destiny. That is a powerful concept.

I doubt that if we decided to usher in a kingdom, we would spend three years solely and intimately pouring into twelve men, one of whom was a betrayer. Yet that is precisely what Jesus did. He knew what it meant to shape a life for destiny.

Dallas Willard, a well-known author and professor of philosophy at the University of Southern California, insists that the world's most significant issue today is authentic discipleship, the kind of discipleship that Jesus taught, modeled, and commissioned. In Willard's book, *The Great*

Omission (based on the evangelical cliché of Matthew 24:29, known as the Great Commission), he writes:

The greatest issue facing the world today, with all its heartbreaking needs, is whether those who, by profession or culture, are identified as "Christians" will become disciples — students, apprentices, practitioners — of Jesus Christ, steadily learning from him how to live the life of the Kingdom of the Heaven into every corner of human existence.

We cannot omit the discipleship commission. Jesus didn't ask us to go into all the world and make Christians, converts, or even church members. He told us to make *mathetes*, Greek for disciples, pupils, and followers of Jesus. He modeled love at the greatest level.

Paul succinctly said, *"Be imitators of me as I am of Christ"* (1 Corinthians 11:1). The Greek word for *imitator* is *mimetes*. It means to follow someone and do what they do. We get our word *mimic* from this Greek word. However, we have turned something so simple, something done for millennia, into a curriculum, a class, and a methodology.

Authentic Discipleship

Allow me to expand on what discipleship is not versus what discipleship is. True discipleship is not:

- A class.
- A curriculum.
- A Bible study group.
- A Sunday morning sermon.
- A prescribed course that lasts for a few weeks, then is over.
- Controlling people.

- Church attendance.

True discipleship, authentic and genuine discipleship, is:

- A lifestyle of interacting with people one-on-one.
- Has no time parameters.
- Expresses genuine concern and love for those the Holy Spirit has brought into your life to influence and train.
- Shares practical truths and life skills Jesus and others have shared with you.
- Allows people to get close enough to you so they can follow your example.
- Loves people with no motivation other than wanting to see them grow and be more like Jesus.
- Shares with people everything you have learned about Jesus, the Bible, and living a Christian life of dignity, character, and maturity.
- Speaks the truth in love without trying to control the disciple.
- Spends one-on-one time with people.
- Invests time, resources, prayer, information, experiences, concern, and, most of all, love in the disciple. It's a kingdom investment with eternal values.

The simple definition of discipleship is doing what Jesus did and modeling what Jesus did. Walk with disciples while they learn to do it, then share with others the same principles. For Jesus, discipleship was a lifestyle, not a class in discipleship. In some cases, discipleship may last hours and, in other cases, years. You, the Holy Spirit, and the disciple determine the time commitment.

Discipleship is a continual reminder of our calling. As the apostle Peter said, *"So I will always remind you of these things, even though you know them and are firmly established in the truth you now have. I think it is right to refresh your memory as long as I live in the tent of this body"* (2 Peter 1:12–13).

Follow Me

Jesus rarely spoke to multitudes. During His final eighteen months of ministry, He spoke to crowds, mostly in the precincts of Jerusalem. But twenty-four seven, for three and a half years, He walked with the disciples, taught them, modeled the Father's life before them, prayed for them in His final hours, and eventually died for them. Discipleship doesn't just tell people what to do; it models the principle in front of them so they can see it and replicate it.

Prayer is one example. Jesus continually prayed. He prayed morning, noon, and night. He prayed early in the morning. He prayed through the night. He prayed three times on His final night. They continually saw and heard Him pray. Though they weren't very good students during His earthly ministry, they became assiduous in their devotion to prayer after His ascension.

I love my wife Devi's quote: "Mentoring invites people into your life and engages all five senses. Teaching, however, only engages hearing and sight, and it's only a one-way conversation."

What did Jesus model for the disciples? He showed them practical kingdom living. He allowed them entrance into His daily life. As John says in the first chapter of his first epistle:

That which was from the beginning, which we have heard, which we have seen with our eyes, which we looked upon and have touched with our hands, concerning the word of life — the life was made manifest, and we have seen it, and testify to it and proclaim to you the eternal life, which was with the Father and was made manifest to us — that which we have seen and heard we proclaim also to you, so that you too may have fellowship with us; and indeed our fellowship is with the Father and with His Son Jesus Christ (1 John 1:1–3).

Notice this verse's many tactile, visual, and auditory descriptions. The disciples heard Him, saw Him, and touched Him physically. The disciples communicated with Jesus, and He with them, very personally. How unlike many teachers of today who are uncomfortable getting to know their students, congregation, or disciples in anything but the most perfunctory, shallow way. As I often say, they love preaching to you on Sunday morning but don't want to have coffee with you on Monday morning.

The Illusion of Perfection

A friend confessed that it was easier for her to speak to packed-out churches than to disciple people individually. She feared that while people loved her teaching, they wouldn't love her if they got to know her intimately. If she kept her distance, she could maintain the illusion of perfection and appear to have all the answers. She vastly underestimated the power of the Holy Spirit to give her the words when she needed them (Luke 12:12) and now prefers one-on-one discipleship. The relationship moves into a new level of authenticity when she remains transparent and unoffended. Discipleship is messy; the disciple is there to grow and learn in an atmosphere of love. We cannot be offended when human nature expresses itself, or we will distance ourselves from people and remove any knowledge of Jesus that person may have known.

From my vantage point, many leaders don't even know how to disciple people. They're afraid of the mess! We are content to preach on Sundays or teach classes where they gather corporately to hear a curriculum. But we're clueless when it comes to walking with people, allowing them to share in our lifestyle, becoming truly acquainted with them, or entering into a mutually edifying relationship. Yet, I can't find another biblical way to train leaders besides discipleship.

I asked one prospective pastor if he would also have home groups when he announced the opening of cell groups in our church. His answer floored me. "Oh, no. We don't like having people over to our home. Our home is only for us." I recommended he reconsider pastoring a church. The home is the most basic and pure form of the church. If you're unwilling to entertain people in your home, you have already indicated your distaste for ministering to the larger body of Christ on a personal level. Plus, it's a qualification for true eldership (1 Timothy 3:1–7).

If we remain aloof from those we are discipling, how will they follow our example? The highest form of discipleship and leadership is that of example, and it is more effective than any other form of teaching. We must model biblical principles, not just preach and teach them.

Our teaching must become practical, walked out in the presence of others tracking behind us.

The first thing Jesus said to the original disciples was, *"Follow me"* (Matthew 4:19), and it works the same way today.

Your First Disciples

The most important form of discipleship is that which takes place in your own home, with your children. After all, home is where the heart is formed. If you have placed ministry on the same level as God to the detriment of your family, what good is that to you? What good is it to love parishioners when your family feels unloved? Your family legacy is the first legacy God gave you to steward and the most important. If you were raised in an environment of abuse and neglect, you have the power to reverse that legacy in your family; how powerful.

Discipleship isn't reserved for just the larger life moments either. When our family was younger, we were given a free vacation to Hawaii. (I wish God would call me as a missionary to Hawaii, don't you?) One night, after our dinner at a fine-dining restaurant, I took advantage of the formal atmosphere to teach my son, who was eight years old at the time, a lesson in etiquette.

"Aaron, when you finish your meal, place your knife and fork in the ten o'clock position on your plate. That will let the waiter know you have finished your meal, and he can remove the plate. It will also position the utensils more securely, so they won't fall off when the plate is removed." Etiquette is very practical.

When I noted his knife in the twelve o'clock position

and the fork in the ten o'clock position, I reached over and moved the knife next to the fork in the ten o'clock position. I repeated, "Aaron, place your silverware in the ten o'clock position so it won't fall off."

Aaron responded, "Why didn't you tell me you wanted it in the ten 'til ten positions?" In his mind, the ten o'clock position was like a literal clock, with the big hand at ten and the small hand at ten. I should have known then that he would eventually become a scientist. My illustration fell flat.

Other hands-on training didn't, however. Everything in daily living becomes an opportunity for discipleship. Listed below are some of the priorities we had in training our children:

- We love Jesus and put Him first in our lives.
- We treat people with love and respect and demand the same of them.
- We teach them to respect authority.
- We teach them to keep their word.
- We train them to pick up their toys and clothes.
- We insist they be on time for their appointments.
- We face crises head-on and deal with them. We don't skirt or evade difficult times.
- We don't allow the children to scream, or even raise their voices, at us or each other. Neither do we allow talking back, disrespect, or sarcasm. Human beings are too tender for sarcasm. The children are also not allowed to say no to instruction.

- We teach that running and playing rough are allowed outdoors, never inside the house.
- We don't jump on the furniture because it destroys an expensive object. The essence of stewardship is to take care of what God gives you.
- When we give them chores, we show them how to do them, working alongside them to model the process.
- Devi and I show love and respect for each other. It's good for your kids to see you kiss and hold hands too.
- We expect their work and homework to be done before they go out to play.
- We read the Bible and obey what it says.
- We don't keep secrets from each other.
- We pray about everything.

A few years ago, I asked my daughter Trina what she considered the most important tip for parenting. "Don't let the siblings fight." And she didn't. Her four kids were never allowed to fight or argue with each other. Today, as adults, they are the most loving siblings you will ever meet.

I asked my son Aaron the same question. His response was, "Be consistent. If you promise to do something, do it."

This is excellent advice for anyone. It's also called "Discipleship 101" and begins at home.

Practical Discipleship

Jonatas Dias is an incredible young leader in Brazil. Johnny and his wife work among the children in the *favelas* (the shantytowns) of Rio De Janeiro. They educate them academically and in the Word of God, disciple them, and give them clothes, food, and toys. In one of his recent S.O.S. Brazil Kids Newsletters, Johnny wrote to his supporters:

I was discipled by a great man who made me believe in discipleship. He taught me that discipleship is showing who you really are in your intimacy and being transparent with those around you with nothing to hide. The best way to teach someone is to walk side by side with that person. Not showing their weaknesses and mistakes but showing how that person can improve in doing the right thing. Emphasizing qualities because, with time, weaknesses will become strengths, and mistakes will become experiences.

Devi was so impressed by Johnny's wisdom that she encouraged him. Johnny replied:

Thank you, Mimi. [Our grandkids, great-grandkids, and now others refer to Devi and me as Mimi and Papa.] *That is what I learned from you and Papa—the day Papa sat down with Matheus and me in the hotel room in California made me understand a different perspective on how to teach someone to do the right thing. The day before, we made many mistakes when he took us to a pastor's house after church for lunch. But the next day, he didn't emphasize what we did wrong. He only told us the right way to behave. And we understood the mistakes we made. It was something automatic in our minds. We didn't feel guilty or that he was putting us down. We felt like we could improve and change to be better.*

Constructive Criticism, Not!

True discipleship doesn't involve showing disciples everything they're doing wrong but what they're doing right. If you build on their strengths, they will improve; if you concentrate on their weaknesses, they will do worse. If you build people up, they will rise to their potential, but if you put them down, they will never reach their potential. Remember, death and life are in the power of the tongue.

I reject the phrase "constructive criticism." I believe all criticism is destructive. You train people by emphasizing their assets and not concentrating on their liabilities. You can make corrections, but they must be approached positively and not negatively, delivered in a spirit of love with your only motivation to assist them in their growth. When instruction is needed, always start first by emphasizing their qualities.

My friend Travis Gates told me of his experience with a professional consultant he'd hired to show him how to improve his work performance. Travis asked the consultant if he wanted to begin with his weaknesses, assuming it was a good place to start.

"No, that's not how we do things," the consultant replied. "We focus on your strengths. As you concentrate on your strengths, the weaknesses become less and fall off. But if you put a microscope on your weaknesses, you will focus on the minors."

I believe that. Somehow, in our humanness, we are often drawn to people's weaknesses before identifying their strengths, and we do the same with ourselves.

In my book, *Lead Differently, Discover How Leading Like Jesus Can Work for You*, I quote the famous German poet and philosopher, Johann Wolfgang von Goethe, who said, "When we treat man as he is, we make him worse than he is; when we treat him as if he already were what he potentially could be, we make him what he should be."

The Bible says, *"Love keeps no record of wrongs"* (1 Corinthians 13:4–6). In a court of law, lawyers ask for specific points to be struck from the record. Essentially, they ask that the statement no longer bear weight on the issue. Rehearsing weaknesses over and over only serves to weaken people. Decide today to clear the record and speak life to others, then watch how your relationships flourish.

Created for Relationship

When God created humankind, He did so within the context of relationships. God declared His entire creation good with one exception: *"It is not good for the man to be alone. I will make a helper suitable for him"* (Genesis 2:18).

Everything that God does involves relationships, and I don't believe God works in any other way. We are a family, the household of God, and that family spirit permeates everything we do. We are not an amorphous entity but the body of Christ, a living organism. As a living, vibrant organism, our teaching should be seeable, teachable, practical, and relational. Our disciples are more than just students listening to our lectures or congregants in pews; they are spiritual sons and daughters with whom we invest our lives. It is our responsibility to draw them into the family circle. No one under our watch should feel like an orphan.

The Father Heart of God

When Jesus related to God, He related to Him as His Father. In the hour of His greatest suffering, He cried out to His Father (Mark 14:36). When He taught His disciples to

pray to God, He taught them to pray to their Father
(Matthew 6:9). The Father sent the Son, empowered by the
Holy Spirit. Likewise, the Son ascended to the Father and
sent the Holy Spirit to empower the body of Christ. The
discipleship model begins with the Father and continues to
reach future generations.

The apostle Paul stressed the importance of fathers
when he said, *"For even if you had ten thousand others to teach
you about Christ, you have only one spiritual father. For I became
your father in Christ Jesus when I preached the Good news to you.
So, I urge you to imitate me"* (1 Corinthians 4:15–16.
Incidentally, this is not a gender issue. As men disciple
younger men, so, Paul says, older women should teach
younger women (Titus 2:4–8). For Paul, true discipleship
involved teaching in the context of family.

With the rapid deterioration of marriage and family, the
world needs spiritual fathers and mothers now, as never
before. It's starved for them. One staff member of a
megachurch told me, "All we ever wanted was a father."
He said it with the plaintive cry of a man who wasn't
getting it. He has since left that staff and is still looking for a
father. He wanted someone more than a mentor
disseminating information. He wanted a spiritual father to
believe in him and do life with him.

After I'd been teaching at a men's conference in Nigeria,
the pastor told me en route to the airport, "You know more
about me and my family in three days than my leader
knows in twenty years." What a sad commentary on the
apostle Paul's words above. What use are "ten thousand"
paid teachers but few fathers?

Before the universe was created, the Father-Son relationship had already existed. From eternity past until eternity future, it is still God's plan that the church be built on relationships. I know this sounds callous and maybe careless, but I believe it is true: Spiritual fathers and mothers are more important in God's plan for the church than paid preachers and teachers. Hebrews 1:1 says, *"Long ago, at many times and in many ways, God spoke to our fathers by the prophets, but in these last days he has spoken to us by his Son, whom he appointed the heir of all things, through whom also he created the world."*

The original Greek omits the word *his*. This makes the verse more emphatic. *"In these last days he has spoken to us by Son."* The Father-Son relationship preempts everything else, forming the foundation for all biblical relationships and training programs. I will state it more firmly: it's impossible to disciple someone with whom you don't have a personal relationship.

God's Desire for Family

It's a simple example, but you plant an apple seed if you want an apple tree. The fruit lies within the seed, a truth found in Genesis 1:11–13 that transcends both the natural and spiritual realms. Galatians 6 teaches that we will reap whatever we sow in the spirit. The seed's death brings the fruit's life, whether natural or supernatural.

God desired an eternal family, and so He gave the seed of His son. *"For God so loved the world, that he gave his only Son, that whoever believes in him should not perish but have eternal life"* (John 3:16). Jesus, in complete harmony with His Father's will, said, *"The hour has come for the Son of Man to be glorified. Truly, truly, I say to you, unless a grain of wheat falls into the earth and dies, it remains alone; but if it dies it bears much fruit"* (John12:23–24). At the cost of His Son, God sent Jesus and at the cost of His life, Jesus died. That is how much God wanted a family.

Hebrews 2:10 says this: *"For it was fitting that he, for whom and by whom all things exist, in bringing many sons to glory, should make the founder of their salvation perfect through suffering."* In this one verse, the purpose of God from eternity is revealed. God was not content to have one Son; His goal was to have many sons and daughters and give His glory to all of them.

To further reiterate heaven's desire for relationships, the writer of Hebrews boldly states that Jesus and the believers have one source: God the Father. This makes us the brethren of Jesus. Wrap your mind around that. Jesus is your Savior, Redeemer, Lord, Intercessor, and Brother. Paul adds another dimension to the divine relationship by stating that we are heirs of God and fellow heirs with Jesus Christ (Romans 8:17). However you slice it, we're family and related.

Having spiritual sons or daughters that you refine and invest in through discipleship brings incredible rewards. I know no better way to make disciples than to allow them into your family and help them be released entirely in their calling. God will use you to bring the very best out in people. The Bible calls it to "glorify" them.

The Power of Affirmation

Please don't underestimate the power of affirmation in setting a person's sails toward their goals. One word, one sentence, one pat on the back for a job well done is more critical for a person's self-esteem than years of training courses.

Twice God spoke out of heaven to affirm His Son. First, in Luke 3:22 NLT: *"You are my dearly loved Son, and you bring me great joy,"* and second, in Luke 9:35 NLT: *"This is my Son, my Chosen One. Listen to him."*

If God found it necessary to affirm His Son to those in attendance at His baptism and transfiguration, how much more do we, as early fathers and mothers, need to affirm our biological and spiritual sons and daughters in front of peers and family?

I've heard it told that Mark Twain said he could live for two months on one good compliment. I believe one good compliment can change a person's life forever. How many children have never heard their parents, or anyone else, say anything encouraging to them? No wonder they have nothing to hang on to.

Words of affirmation are necessary to give young disciples the courage to pursue their dreams. And some of those occasions should be public.

After the morning service ended, I was talking with a group of men in the church foyer when one of their fathers walked over. I immediately took the opportunity to validate his son and let the father know how special he was. This was no ordinary young man; he was exceptional in every way. I was so excited to share how highly I esteemed him in the presence of his friends and dad.

"You're Joe's dad? I'm so glad to meet you. Your son is awesome, and he's incredible. I'm thrilled to meet you." What a perfect time to validate his son amid his peers.

Sadly, the father responded, "Well, it's obvious you don't know him like I do." I immediately saw the countenance on his son's face drop. We all just stood there, not knowing what to do. What should have been the perfect setup to edify his son publicly became uncomfortable, embarrassing, and soured because of the dad's thoughtless and insensitive response. No one knew what to say.

My first thought was, "I gave you the perfect opportunity to affirm your son in the company of his friends, and you blew it." My second was, "How can I get to his son in time to reverse the curse of that open rejection?" Fortunately, the son had enough courage to confront his dad later in the week, and the dad apologized.

God has called us to glorify our sons and daughters and spiritual sons and daughters. Bring them open honor and encourage them. Brag on them, like the Father bragged on His Son:

"Now when all the people were baptized, and when Jesus also had been baptized and was praying, the heavens were opened, and the Holy Spirit descended on him in bodily form, like a dove, and a voice came from heaven, 'You are my beloved Son; with you I am well pleased'" (Luke 3:21–22 ESV).

Continually Seek to Promote Others

I've never understood why believers envy one another's success in the kingdom of God. Why not offer their resources to each other? This is not about building our kingdom; it's about building God's. Why not allow someone to stand on your shoulders to reach higher? Purposefully position yourself as a tool God uses to release their greatness.

A few weeks ago, I received a letter from a pastor in Washington State who had spoken at our church as a teenager. I knew I was taking a risk, allowing an eighteen-year-old to speak while I was on vacation, but I was confident in his abilities and anointing. Enclosed within his letter was one I had written to him, dated September 14, 1970, following his ministry to the church:

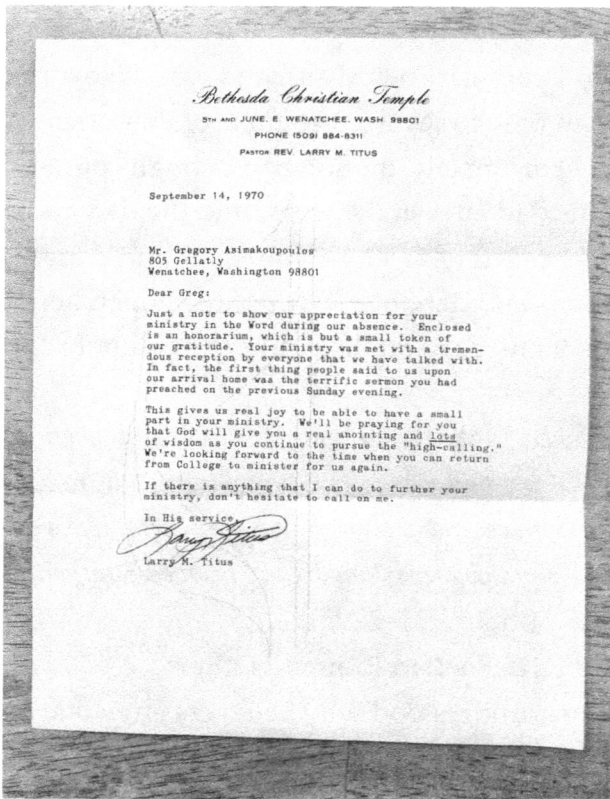

This young man became a great pastor, theologian, and author. Greg Asimakoupoulos is still an influential leader in the body of Christ. I can take little credit for his success, but maybe this early encouragement became a catalyst for greater things. Young ministries grow faster when encouraged and affirmed and investing in children, and youth bears fruit beyond our expectations in their adulthood. As Jesus proves, discipleship is the world's most effective form of training.

The Extraordinary Ordinary

We live in a culture that teaches us to derive pleasure by jumping from one exciting experience to the next or from one high to the other. In this environment, life's simple pleasures are often overlooked, relegated as mundane and boring. However, extraordinary things happen when we invite others into our everyday lives and model Jesus' values by doing life together. 1 Thessalonians 4:11–12 in the NIV says, *"make it your ambition to lead a quiet life: You should mind your own business and work with your hands, just as we told you, so that your daily life may win the respect of outsiders and so that you will not be dependent on anybody."*

There are two additional letters I'd like to share by way of example. The first is from Aaron Cho, a man that I have discipled since 2010:

I grew up attending church and even had a few encounters with the Lord in my youth, but I never knew how to follow Him. I believed the basics of the gospel because I had memorized John 3:16 in Sunday School, but that was pretty much it. Due to my shallow understanding of the gospel, my faith wasn't relevant in my life during high school, college, or as a young professional. I worked hard and played harder—drinking, partying, and living in sexual immorality. But God never gave up on me.

At age twenty-four, I indeed committed my life to Christ. As a management consultant in San Francisco, I traveled extensively for business and was assigned to an eight-month engagement in Dallas, Texas. In the spring of 2010, I boarded a flight to Dallas and met Devi and Larry Titus, which forever changed my life and family legacy.

During my extended stay in Dallas, Larry discipled me. He welcomed me into his life. He invited me to his home for meals, late evening coffees, and TV dates, just lounging on the sofa. He asked me to the grocery store while he went shopping for Devi. There was no agenda involved; we did movies together, Mexican food, department stores—you name it, wherever Dad has walked, I've probably walked with him. The fun, the mundane, the normalcy of life…I've experienced it all with Larry (Dad) Titus.

When he visited San Francisco to guest preach at a church, he would reach out, and we would connect. On another visit to the Bay Area, where he and Devi were visiting family, Dad took me to Carmel, CA, to walk the white sand beach town and Monterey to enjoy a seafood lunch on Cannery Row. Dad would buy me gifts on my birthday, which was a shocker since nobody outside my family knew my birthday. Just like John 21:25, when the apostle John notes that it would be impossible for all the books in the world to contain everything Jesus did, I don't think this one-page testimonial could hold everything Dad invited me to. I've attended formal and informal engagements with him and all the holiday events.

To me, Larry wasn't just a preacher or teacher. He was far more—he became my "Dad" and adopted me into his spiritual family. At the beginning of our relationship, I expected him to teach me in a traditional sense. I thought he would share his vast Bible knowledge with me. And though he's undoubtedly done that *during the last thirteen-plus years of our relationship, his method of discipleship (which mirrors that of Jesus) was far more effective. Dad invited me to follow him as he followed Christ. Getting to know Dad better made me want to know Jesus better. When I asked him for guidance, he asked me what the Holy Spirit said. He didn't control me; he directed me to whom he was following.*

Dad was far more interested in my life than in sharing his theology. He allowed me (and eventually my wife and kids) into his life and his family. After marrying my wife, Miran, we got a front-row seat in the Discipleship 101 course. I saw how Dad served Devi and cared for her like a precious jewel. He did the dishes, opened the car door, and did countless other acts of service for Devi. I wanted to do the same for my bride. Dad showed me photos of his multigenerational Christ-following family, whom I met. I desired the same legacy.

He said he was proud of me when I hadn't accomplished much. He called me a pastor when I was in the marketplace. He said I was awesome when I sometimes didn't feel so awesome. Spending time with Dad was like spending time with Jesus. I felt loved and affirmed and gained confidence in God's love and purpose for my life. Dad Titus reflected the Heavenly Father's love and thoughts for me in a very tangible way.

Over the years, our relationship has grown into a Paul and Timothy type of relationship. He's watched me grow into a complete man—a follower of Christ, a husband, a father, and a marketplace leader. I'm forever grateful for his influence and impartation, and I can't wait for my next breakfast meeting with him (which, in current 2023, is a weekly occasion). No agenda, no lesson. Just Father and Son time.

Occasionally the father/son discipleship takes a hiatus,

whereby for some reason, there is a season of noninvolvement. Such is the case with Jeff Hamilton, a young man from our early ministry. Life events separated us for many years, only to be restored in the past decade to the point where Jeff has become a major contributor to several books I have written during the past decade. This is Jeff's story:

It was a dark, wet night in Los Angeles, and I was driving home after a long day at work. Before leaving, I took a pill timed to put me to sleep once I arrived home, but instead, it made me dizzy. I pulled over and stood beside some reeking garbage containers to get my bearings, but my balance faltered, and I fell and hit my head. After lying on the greasy blacktop, I roused myself and drove toward my home with a throbbing, bleeding head.

I was only a few blocks from the house I'd recently purchased. But the city was new to me, and coupled with the rain and my injury, I was soon lost in the complex streets of Los Angeles.

The week before, I'd learned the girlfriend I'd been living with for a few years was seeing an old lover. I was about to lose the prestigious job I had come to California for due to a corporate purchase, and I was running low on cash. And now I feared the cops would pull me over for drunk driving. A Southern California tidal wave of despair and confusion began to wash over me.

I was reeling and desperate. I needed a life raft, but where to call for help? My parents were still alive. I had good friends and brothers and sisters. But I needed more. I was over my head.

Peering through the rainy windshield, it came to me. I needed to find my pastor from Washington State—the guy who had spent several years in my hometown disciplining me. Where was Larry Titus? I knew he was living somewhere back on the East Coast, but it was late, and I didn't like to call people late at night. Nonetheless, I called him without a second thought or shame, hoping he would show a little mercy to a wayward son. Larry answered the phone.

Fifteen years prior, I'd left my hometown in Washington State to finish school. Thanks to help from nearly everyone I knew, including Larry, things went well for me. I accumulated significant degrees and big jobs, little knowing I was headed into my perfect storm.

Before I left town for school, Larry became a trusted, consistent father figure and coach. He showed me how to do innumerable things in this new world of faith. He and Devi even took me into their house, where I lived for months. I saw firsthand what living a Christ-centered life was all about.

A seminary formed at the booming church Larry had founded, and I attended some of the classes. I'd never worked so hard in an academic setting and did well.

But I hadn't done well with Jesus. Many of those years were like the night I fell by the Los Angeles garbage cans and hit my head. Ambition and the endless conceits of corporate life pulled me away from what had become near and dear to me. I got way ahead of myself. Disaster waited like a troll under the bridge.

I'd been saved and filled with the Holy Spirit in Larry's office. He mentored me in a near-apprenticeship way. He took me and others he mentored nationwide to music and teaching ministries. I smile, remembering all the impromptu lunch invitations, the racquetball sessions, and the discussions with young leaders. We gathered and prayed at any given time in his living room. His family was in synch with his heart and would graciously welcome us into their household.

Other leaders in my life always maintained a better version of themselves around those they coached or led, withheld selected parts of their lives, and displayed a public face to their charges. Not so with Larry.

Larry taught with his life—how he washed his car, showed love and respect to his family, and gave things to others. (The real gift was his time.) I remember how we brazenly imitated him. We picked up his speech inflections, prayed like him, adopted his gestures, and studied Scripture as he did. More importantly, we began to believe like him and nurture our relationships with Jesus Christ.

A craftsman once told me, "Learning is through the skin." We learn something by doing it. Holding the tool to the leather makes us feel the work through our fingers. That's how Larry taught us. So, my time with Larry had been authentic and unconditional. I gained enormous respect and trust for him. That's the best way I can describe it. That's why I called him in the middle of the night that year from Los Angeles.

Larry instantly and immediately came to my help. He didn't ask for context as to where I was living or what I was doing. That came later. He heard the terror in my voice and did triage and damage control. In the months and years to follow, he continued to mentor me. I went to towns where he was speaking, seminars, and teaching events, and I met people I would never have met— people who have helped me along the way. We'd have lunch when he was in town, and once again, I got to hear his fantastic teaching. However, I have learned more from how Larry mentored than I have through any doctrine he taught us. When I read the

Scriptures, I see that Larry's compassion and faithfulness mirror Jesus' way with the disciples.

Discipleship: An Investment of the Heart

Living life with others and remaining steadfast in their lives is key. No matter where their lives lead, their ups and downs or highs and lows, remain steadfast. Jesus' perfect discipleship model will always remain the most authentic way to lead people to Him.

My friend mentors many women who constantly seek her opinion. She responds, "My opinion and three bucks can get you a cup of coffee." In other words, "My advice isn't worth much." She knows that if she advises without modeling the process of hearing God, the women will never learn to hear for themselves. And so, she spends time *with* them, prays *with* them, and asks the Holy Spirit to speak directly *to* them. Together they wait on His answer and talk about it, weighing what the women have heard with the Scriptures. When the mentoring season ends, the women no longer ask her opinion; they feel confident hearing directly from the Holy Spirit because they learned *how to* during the discipleship process. Building this type of confidence in people takes time, patience, and love. It is an investment of the heart.

Paul said it this way: *"Therefore, my brothers and sisters, you whom I love and long for, my joy and crown, stand firm in the Lord in this way, dear friends!"* (Philippians 4:1, NIV). When we begin to see people as our crown, the reason behind our every motive, and a source of love and joy, we have discovered the true heart of discipleship.

Resources

There are several excellent books on discipleship I encourage you to read:

Call to Discipleship and *Disciple* (also available in Spanish) by Juan Carlos Ortiz. Though out of print, they are two of the finest works I've ever read on this topic, with invaluable illustrations. I'm sure you can still get his used books on the internet. Though written decades ago, they are still germane and apropos to this generation.

Contagious Disciple Making, by David L. Watson and Paul D. Watson, is on planting and shepherding disciple-based churches. Years of effective church planting make this book invaluable.

My book *LEAD Differently: Discover How Leading Like Jesus Can Work for You* is available from Amazon. One chapter is devoted to Jesus' discipleship principles, and many other chapters reveal details of the process involved. My book *Complete Man* also has a chapter on discipleship.

CHAPTER 4
PURSUE UNITY IN THE BODY OF CHRIST

"That they may all be one, just as you, Father are in me, and I in you, that they also may be in us, so that the world may believe that you have sent me" (John 17:21).

"I therefore, a prisoner for the Lord, urge you to walk in a manner worthy of the calling to which you have been called, with all humility and gentleness, with patience, bearing with one another in love, eager to maintain the unity of the Spirit in the bond of peace" (Ephesians 4:1–3).

Psalm 133:1–3 states, *"Behold, how good and pleasant it is when brothers dwell in unity! It is like the precious oil on the head, running down on the beard, on the beard of Aaron, running down on the collar of his robes! It is like the dew of Hermon, which falls on the mountains of Zion!"* In the Old Testament, we learn that Mount Zion is none other than the dwelling place of God (Isaiah 8:18). Take a moment to picture this. In His kingdom, fresh dew cools the grass, and fragrant priestly oil made of myrrh and cinnamon (Exodus 30:22–25) delights the senses as it pours from the head of His high priest. The image is one of abundance, emanating peace and brimming with life.

Contrast this to Jesus' warning about division in Matthew 12:25: *"Every kingdom divided against itself is laid waste, and no city or house divided against itself will stand."* The Greek for *waste* is *eremos* and means wilderness or desolation resulting in isolation. In this scenario, division lays an entire kingdom to waste, devastating cities and homes. The image of a lifeless wasteland contrasts sharply with Psalm 133. No wonder the enemy sows seeds of discord and confusion among God's people (Matthew 13:24–25). He wants to destroy God's peaceful kingdom, causing havoc and isolation. God declared that it was not good for man to be alone (Genesis 2:18), and that's precisely what division brings. Aloneness.

The Value of Unity

Paul is notorious for penning some of the longest sentences in the Bible. It's as if he is worried that he will forget what he was trying to say if he stops writing. Ephesians 4 has several such sentences. The underlying theme is unity in the church, the body of Christ.

I want to quote these verses, but doing so requires that I pick up the sentence several lines earlier. The verses that highlight unity are in bold.

*I therefore, a prisoner for the Lord, urge you to walk in a manner worthy of the calling to which you have been called, with all humility and gentleness, with patience, bearing with one another in love, **eager to maintain the unity of the Spirit in the bond of peace.***

*There is **one** body and **one** Spirit—just as you were called to the **one** hope that belongs to your call—**one** Lord, **one** faith, **one** baptism, **one** God and Father of all, who is over all and through all and in all* (Ephesians 4:1–6).

Ephesians 4:11–16 says,

*And he gave the apostles, the prophets, the evangelists, the shepherds and teachers, to equip the saints for the work of ministry, for building up the body of Christ, **until we all attain to the unity of the faith** and of the knowledge of the Son of God, to mature manhood, to the measure of the stature of the fullness of Christ, so that we may no longer be children, tossed to and fro by the waves and carried about by every wind of doctrine, by human cunning, by craftiness in deceitful schemes. Rather, speaking the truth in love, we are **to grow up in every way into him who is the head**, into Christ, from whom the whole body, joined and held together by every joint with which it is equipped, when each part is working properly, makes the body grow so that it builds itself up in love.*

Whew! Paul finally finished the sentence. If Paul's sermons were as long as his sentences, it's no wonder Eutychus fell out of the window during his sermon in Troas and died. I nearly fell asleep typing this.

But I want you to reread it, carefully noting how highly God values unity and how it is produced and sustained. It's an eternal principle. The whole purpose of the body of Christ is to grow up into the maturity of its Head, Jesus Christ. The church today looks more like a shriveled body attached to a mature head. We cannot grow into maturity without unity. As long as we remain divided, we will forever live a diminished spiritual life, unable to assimilate into the maturity of our Head. God the Father, Son, and Spirit expect us to replicate their purpose in everything. This applies to the church and marriage, which I will discuss later in the chapter.

A Harmonious Symphony

We don't fully understand how division negatively affects our lives, churches, marriages, and society. Neither do we fully comprehend the power of unity. Jesus said that if two agree about anything, the Father would answer their prayers (Matthew 18:19).

The word *agree* in Matthew 18:19 is *symphoneo* in Greek. We get our word *symphony* from this word. A symphony is a mixture of harmonious sounds. Its opposite is a *cacophony*, a combination of discordant, harsh sounds. The church has two problems in this context. The first is that we don't know how to produce symphonies, and the second is that we are often part of the contentious, cacophonous, divisive crowd that only knows how to whine, argue, and complain about things, ensuring nothing gets done. I'm sure many of these people are on the church board.

To produce a symphony, we must reject solos. Most leaders only know how to perform solos. The only person they can work with is themselves. If it isn't their idea, they won't cooperate. If it's not an idea that builds their kingdom, they won't participate. If they can't control it, they won't get involved. All these patterns mitigate against unity and are carnal.

The Diversity of Unity

Unity can only be established and maintained if the leader is more interested in symphonies than solos. To

THE ACCESS TO POWER

produce unity in any group or project, diversity must be appreciated. It is impossible to obtain agreement when there is sameness. If everyone must have the same skin color, doctrinal consensus, homogeneous cultural bend, and unquestionably follow the leader, there can be sameness but not unity. One of anything cannot produce unity. Unity demands diversity.

The Greek word for *unity* is *henotace,* meaning unanimity or agreement, never sameness. It is from the root word *heis,* meaning *one.* For anything or anyone to unite, there must be diversity of participants but sameness of purpose. For some reason, leaders tend to pressure people into hegemony and sameness and are uncomfortable with diversity. Many fear diversity. It's unnerving to them. But without diversity, there can be no unity. We would not have to work toward unity if we were all the same.

God loves diversity. Have you seen the underwater world? Have you ever scuba dived or snorkeled among the reefs? Have you seen the sizes, shapes, and colors of the animal world? Have you witnessed the diversity of people in the world? Billions of people on the earth, and not one is like another.

Diversity is modeled after the Trinity, where no member of the Trinity has the same personality, yet all work in tandem and agreement to bring cohesion to God's family.

In Colossians 1:17, Paul says, *"And He is before all things, and in him all things **hold together**."* The Greek word for *hold together* is *sunistao.* It is comprised of two words: *sun* and *histemi. Sun* (pronounced *soon*) means *together,* and *histemi* means *to stand.* It is used only sixteen times in the New

Testament and means *to stand together*. It has this meaning in Luke 9:32, where Peter, James, and John stand together with Jesus in His transfiguration.

It also means *to exist*. It is used this way in 2 Peter 3:5 and Colossians 1:17, quoted above. The meaning is simple: When Jesus created the world in all its diversity, He created it so it would cohere, stick together, form a cohesion, a united whole. Everything God does exists in harmony— everything the devil does results in confusion, friction, division, secession, and hatred.

According to the Center for the Study of Global Christianity, there are forty-five thousand denominations worldwide, numbering over two billion believers. Many churches have split on multiple occasions. We have even divided our divisions. In-house fighting is everywhere. Politics runs rampant throughout the church. Corruption and immorality are ubiquitous. We have gone from being one in Christ to thousands of divisions, each claiming to be correct. I can't imagine a more significant blight on the body of Christ. It appears we cannot come together or unify even in one area.

A pastor from San Francisco told me that the church he pastored had been through forty-two church splits. Can you imagine that? Forty-two churches were planted out of that one church through division. Christ never intended the church to grow through division.

In 1 Corinthians 11, Paul rebukes the church for their divisive ways when partaking in the Lord's Supper. Again, in 1 Corinthians 3, Paul quickly points out that in-house fighting over leadership precipitates the Corinthian church's strife and jealousy. The people were unwilling to admit that both he and Apollos were just servants of Jesus Christ, and that Christ alone was foundational to the church.

I'm sorry to be so theological in this chapter, but maybe I'm not. Perhaps I need to be. One of the other Greek words Paul uses at the beginning of his plea for unity in Ephesians 4:3 is *spoudazo*. We must be "**eager** to maintain the unity in the bond of peace." The word *spoudazo*, translated as *eager*, means to make haste, hurry up, and be zealous. It's a very forceful word. We must hurry, speed up, and be zealous to maintain unity in the body of Christ. It's a priority—a mandate, a "hurry up," a *spoudazo*. That's how critical it is.

Let's get serious. It's time we stop fighting, dividing, politicking, competing, bickering, and envying. It's time we stop tearing down other ministries and begin to build them. It's time we appreciate diversity, people that look different, sound different, believe differently, dress differently, and act other than us. God loves harmony. Division is more than petty, it's deadly, and no church body can grow unless it is dealt with.

Areas of Growth to Actively Pursue Unity through Diversity

- Value the opinions of others who see things differently than you.
- Attend and cooperate with other churches and events you didn't sponsor.
- Be open to change.
- Pursue racial diversity in your ministry.

- Attend conferences that are not of your denominational family.
- Center your unity on the cross of Christ, not on differences in doctrine.
- Invite people to your home who are not your usual friends.
- Speak only words of edification about other ministers and churches.
- Rid yourself of all forms of bias and prejudice.
- Invite people of other races to speak at your church.
- Though you should teach biblical principles, keep politics out of your church.
- Get acquainted with your public officials, ensuring they don't "use" you for political gain.
- Read books that present a different view on things.
- Include generational diversity in your events.

The greatest example of unity is God Himself. We call it the Trinity. While the word *Trinity* per se is not found in the Bible, the principle of our triune God is seen throughout. The Father, Son, and Holy Spirit are one in **purpose** but never one in **person**.

The administrative differences in the personalities of the Godhead are multitudinous. To name a few:

Concerning the Father and Son

- The Father is immortal. The Son chose mortality for a time when He dwelt in a mortal body and died on the cross (1 Timothy 1:17; 6:15–16). The Father cannot die, and the Son did (1 Timothy 1:17; 6:16).

- The Father is invisible, and the Son is visible (Colossians 1:15; 1 Timothy 1:17; 6:15–16).
- No one can see the Father and live (Exodus 33:20). Thousands of people saw the Son. Multitudes saw and touched Christ throughout the Gospels (1 John 1:1; 1 Corinthians 15:5–6).
- Jesus is seated at the Father's right hand, and the Father sits on the central throne (Ephesians 1:20; Colossians 3:1; Hebrews 1:3, 13; Revelation 3:21).
- God puts the enemies of Jesus under His feet, not vice versa (Ephesians 1:22; Hebrews 1:13; 10:13; 1 Corinthians 15:25; Luke 20:42–43).
- Jesus is called the Lamb of God; the Father is not (John 1:29; 1 Peter 1:19; Revelation 5:6).
- Jesus prayed to the Father; the Father did not pray to the Son (John 17).
- Jesus was "begotten" of the Father, not vice versa (John 1:14; 3:16).
- Jesus "became flesh," God incarnate. (John 1:14) God the Father will also dwell, or
- "tabernacle," among us in the New Jerusalem, events at least two thousand years apart (Revelation 21:3).
- Jesus had an earthly mother. God the Father has none (Luke 1:31–35).
- God the Father is called the Most High God, and Jesus is called His Son (Luke 1:32).

- The Father put the sins of the world on the Son, not vice versa (2 Corinthians 5:21).
- Jesus spoke only the words and did only the works the Father gave Him. Not vice versa (John 5:19).
- Neither angels nor Jesus know the time of Jesus' return, only the Father (Matthew 24:36).
- Jesus said the Father was greater than Him (John 14:28).
- When the kingdom of God is fully realized, Jesus subjects Himself to the Father, and the Father becomes all in all (1 Corinthians 15:28).
- The Son received dominion, glory, and kingdom from God the Father, known in Daniel 7 as the Ancient of Days (Daniel 7:14).

Concerning the Holy Spirit

- He could only come to dwell once Jesus ascended to the Father following His resurrection (John 7:37–39).
- Jesus asked the Father for "another" Helper (John 16:7).
- He alone of the Trinity can be blasphemed (Mark 3:29).
- He alone provides a Tabernacle of God inside the believer (1 Corinthians 3:16; 6:19).
- People are born again through the agency of the Spirit (John 3:3, 5–6).

- People are baptized into the body of Christ by the Holy Spirit (1 Corinthians 12:13).
- He is the power of God in the believer (Acts 1:8).
- In Romans 8:11, He is the member of the Godhead that raised Jesus from the dead and will raise believers from the dead
- He is the member of the Godhead to intercede within the believer on this earth (John 14:16, 26; 15:26; Romans 8:26).
- He is the member of the Trinity that convicts the world of sin, convinces them of the Spirit, and reveals the reality of the judgment to them (John 16:7–11).
- He is a special gift (*dorea* in Greek) to the believer, separate from the Father and the Son (Acts 2:38.
- He alone of the Trinity is never described as having corporeal features. He is represented as wind, breath, dove, water, fire, etc.
- He administrates the will of God from this earth, not heaven.
- He has fruit (Galatians 5:22–23).
- He has gifts (1 Corinthians 12).
- He can fill believers with the power of God (Acts 1:8).

I could mention numerous other Scriptures that show the difference in personality and administrative tasks assigned to each of the members of the Trinity, but the whole point in citing these Scriptures is to show you that each member of the Trinity is totally unique yet absolutely unified in purpose, mutual edification, and selfless adoration. They work in tandem but are distinct. Together, they give the ultimate example of what God desires of us. God wants all His creation to work in unity. That is why Paul says in Ephesians 4 that there is **one** Body, **one** Spirit, **one** baptism, **one** hope, **one** Lord, and **one** Father. God wants everything to operate in unity. But you cannot have unity without diversity. Sameness does not produce unity; only diversity can do that.

Unity Obtained through Headship

To obtain unity, we must understand the principle of headship. The same principles that bring unity in the church also apply to marriage, the marketplace, society, the military, and the government. Below are seven aspects of headship that result in unity.

1. Headship must be established first.

The first question to ask is, "Who is in charge?" Unity can never be accomplished without that question being asked first.

In the church, the answer is easy. God the Father is the Head of all creation, and Jesus the Son is the Head of the church. As Jesus does the will of the Father, so we do the will of Jesus. There is only one Head of the church, and His name is Jesus. We line up behind only one person, and it's the Commander of the Armies of the Lord, Jesus Christ. Paul is not the head of the church. Apollos is not the head of the church, Larry is not the head of the church, the pope is not the head of the church, your pastor is not the head of the church, and most importantly, you are not the head of the church.

In marriage, Paul said the man is the head of the wife, as Christ is the head of the church. I have one entire book on this topic, *When Leaders Live Together*, and a chapter in my book for men, *The Complete Man*.

1 Corinthians 11:3 states, "*But I want you to understand that the head of every man is Christ, the head of a wife is her husband, and the head of Christ is God.*" In Ephesians, Paul puts it this way: "*For the husband is the head of the wife even as Christ is the head of the church, his body, and is himself its Savior*" (Ephesians 5:23).

There would be far less grasping and grappling for authority if everyone understood headship. The word for *head* in Greek is *kephale*. While it can be a metaphor for many things, the typical usage (over seventy times in the New Testament) is that part of the anatomy that sits on top of the body, supported by the neck, and is the seat of intellect, imagination, and memory, and gives direction to the body.

It's not my purpose to go into detail right now as to how this should operate in marriage but to explain how it **must** work in the church. There can be no ambiguity on this point.

The Head of Jesus is God.

The Head of the church is Jesus.

Regardless of your ecclesiastical position, you are NOT the head of the church. Only Jesus is. Stop fighting over who is more important, Paul or Peter. The answer is neither. This means, practically speaking, that the church must confer with its Head in every situation to gain direction. And you, as a leader in the church, must defer to the will of the Head, Jesus.

Too often, pastors and church leaders are swayed by the opinions of the members in the pew rather than the Head, who is at the Father's right hand. It would be best to decide based on what heaven says rather than what the members clamor for. I've seen churches split over the color of the carpet. Better not to have carpet.

1. The head must embrace diversity.

Wise leaders will also allow for diversity of opinion and diversity of participants. If you think you've achieved unity because you all look and think alike, you're sadly mistaken.

1. The head must set the direction.

It is not up to the body to decide where to go. The leader must determine the destination, or there will be mass confusion. As a leader in the church, you cannot possibly know the direction you or the flock should take without spending time in prayer, asking the Head, Jesus Christ, for clarity of His will.

Goals must be identified. Where are you going? Paul gives a great illustration when discussing the appropriate use of tongues in 1 Corinthians 14:8. *"If the trumpet gives an indistinct sound, who will prepare for battle?"* Too many goals and visions lack clear direction and purpose. Whoever sounds the trumpet needs to give a clarion call, or troops won't assemble to engage in battle. I'm unwilling to follow a leader who doesn't know where they are going.

The prophet Habakkuk stationed himself upon a watchtower to hear what the Lord would say to him. The Lord said, *"Write the vision, make it plain on tablets, so he may run who reads it"* (Habakkuk 2:2). It means to write your vision on a billboard so everyone who runs by will see it and spread the vision. God's messages are never confusing but concise, convincing, and creative.

1. The head must release the people in their areas of gifting.

Unless the head (leader) wants to handle all tasks alone, they must delegate responsibility to all the participants or members. We have too many churches with big heads and little bodies; they micromanage and do everything themselves.

Leaders should judge how successful their project was by how many people were actively involved in carrying the weight of the project, not by how much money was raised. Every member needs to be involved and feel part of the process. Sometimes, the most successful campaigns are when volunteers carry out the project. Don't ever underestimate or undervalue volunteers.

1. The head must earnestly pray for unity.

If Jesus spent time praying for unity in His final prayer on earth, it would behoove us to have the same attitude. In

John 17:21, Jesus prayed, *"That they all may be one, just as you, Father, are in me, and I in you, that they also may be in us, so that the world may believe that you have sent me."* I believe the world will never be convinced that the Father sent Jesus until the church comes into unity. Let's pray that the forty-five thousand denominations and two billion believers will become one in Christ.

1. The head must find qualified administrators who add structure to the vision.

Often, projects fail for a lack of preparation rather than a lack of vision. In the following verse, Habakkuk 2:3 reveals how to succeed in fulfilling the vision: *"For still the vision awaits its appointed time; it hastens to the end — it will not lie. If it seems slow, wait for it; it will surely come; it will not delay."*

The key is patience. Every project requires the specific elements of organization, administration, timing, and fulfillment. Or, as Jesus put it, don't start building a tower unless you have the material and money to complete it. Or don't go to battle without knowing you have enough strength, firepower, and ammunition to win the war (Luke 14:28).

If you're going to ask people to follow your vision, you must make clear the cost. There can be **no** surprises. I know of one fundraising campaign where people were asked to prayerfully write down their financial contributions for budgeting purposes and bring them to a church service. When the people arrived, the leaders said, "Now take those papers and ask God if this is really your best." Talk about an unpleasant surprise. Many people left the service feeling confused and manipulated. Pledges were upped out of guilt and never fulfilled.

Vision can only come to fruition with thorough preparation. Failure to complete your projects will dissipate your support base. Unity comes when people are of one purpose, one head (leader), one attitude, one passion, and one direction.

1. The head must be prepared to take responsibility.

In Genesis 3, Adam abdicated his role as head of his wife. Rather than partaking with her of the forbidden fruit, he should have been prepared to pay the price of her deception. Instead, Jesus, the Head of the church and affectionately called the "second Adam" (1 Corinthians 15:45–49) who committed no sin, ultimately paid the price.

President Truman famously had a sign on his desk that read, "The buck stops here." In other words, he was prepared to accept all responsibility for his decision-making without placing blame. Blame and shame are closely related. There are times when, as a leader, you must take responsibility for things you did not do, trusting God to sort them out. This is the Christlike posture of humility reflected in Philippians 2: *"Have this mind among yourselves, which is yours in Christ Jesus, who though he was in the form of God, did not count equality with God a thing to be grasped, but made himself nothing, taking the form of a servant."* This attitude reflects a complete emptying of self, not caring for your right to be right.

In short, we need more symphonies and far fewer solos in the body of Christ.

The Power of Unity

In April 1831, a brigade of soldiers marched in step across England's Broughton Suspension Bridge. According to accounts of the time, the bridge broke apart beneath the soldiers, resulting in dozens of men being thrown into the water. After this, the British Army reportedly sent new orders: Soldiers crossing a long bridge must "break stride," or not march in unison, to stop the situation from occurring again.

Even though bridges and buildings appear solid and immovable, they have a natural vibration frequency within them. Mechanical resonance occurs when the force applied to an object at the same frequency as its natural frequency amplifies its vibration.

Can you imagine what could happen if the body of Christ came together in one accord, as they did on the day of Pentecost? Can you imagine the explosive power that would be released if we marched in unison, determined to destroy the works of the enemy?

What if we were to make one sound in praising the Lord, as they did in Solomon's temple dedication? When the Levitical singers, the musicians with their cymbals, harps, and lyres, and the 120 priests blew their trumpets, singing and playing in unison, "*For he is good, for his steadfast love endures forever*" (2 Chronicles 5:13), the temple was filled with the glory of the Lord. My heart yearns for this to happen in the church.

Unity in Marriage

I firmly believe unity begins in the home, with the husband and wife walking together. If unity doesn't occur there, how can we expect it to happen in the church? If you are married, the DNA of your marriage partnership will be replicated in the church.

After nearly fifty-nine years of marriage, I am convinced many Christian couples have never experienced the joy of walking in unity. They compete, fight, argue, and dishonor each other. They don't live biblically with the husband as the head of the marriage and the wife in submission to his headship. Often, the wife is the head of the marriage.

In other cases, the husband has never learned to serve and honor his wife. The husband is a dictatorial leader whom the rest of the family completely disdains, beginning with the wife. He doesn't look like Jesus, and the wife doesn't look like the future bride of Christ. They live lives of division and hostility. They never become one and never know the joy of living in unity. How can we be deceived into thinking this will not be reflected in how we treat our church members?

Devi and I cannot remember a time we fought. Yes, we have had disagreements, but we talk them out. Neither of us is interested in winning. Marriage isn't a battle, and my spouse isn't my enemy. We have spent our entire marriage honoring and serving each other. Why would I dishonor the most precious person in the world? Why would I say words that would injure her? As Devi told our family on Christmas Eve, four days before she died, December 28,

2022, "Larry and I have never intentionally hurt each other." I can't even write this without crying.

Do you know what it means to live with another person for nearly sixty years and never intentionally injure another person? I'll tell you what it's like. When your spouse passes away, it feels as though half of you died. There is no way I can describe it. It's a massive hole that only Jesus can fill.

We lived our marriage with the words of Jesus preeminent in our hearts when He quoted Genesis 2:24 in Matthew 19:4–5: *"Have you never read that he who created them from the beginning made them male and female, and said, 'Therefore a man shall leave his father and his mother and hold fast to his wife, and the two shall become one flesh?'"*

I've seen couples married for fifty years that have never come into unity. They live in the same house but never become one. The husband goes one way and the wife the other. Children have their agenda and schedule, and it doesn't include either parent. They don't know how to live as a family, as a unit, as one in spirit. What a heartbreak.

Please, please, please consider your marriage as a priority. If your marriage isn't a priority, it's unlikely your church will be healthy. I'm speaking to men: if you don't honor and edify your wife, neither will your children. I'm speaking to women: if you don't honor and edify your husband, your children will treat their father with contempt and disrespect, which will be your fault.

Like the Trinity, God expects us to honor, respect, prefer, serve, and love each other as they have done from eternity. That is what makes them one. You will not become one in unity if the only time you're one is when you're having sex.

This lifestyle is a daily, deliberate attempt to prefer the other above yourself. If marriage teaches you anything, it teaches that to live a life of peace and dignity, you must live selflessly. Selfish living is a marriage destroyer.

I know this isn't a book on marriage, but I would be remiss if I didn't make one more point. As noted above, nothing can come into unity without diversity. You must appreciate the differences between you and your spouse rather than despise them. Of course, she is different than you. Of course, he is different from you. That was designed by God. You need to be grateful for those differences. They are necessary for the marriage to work.

Most likely, what you are good at, your spouse isn't. And the opposite is true. Whatever they excel in is most likely a weakness in your personality. That's God's way of causing both of you to excel. Don't despise it but embrace it. Be grateful for it. It gives you a much greater chance of success. The Old Testament says one can put a thousand to flight, but two can put ten thousand to flight (Deuteronomy 32:30).

You cannot have unity without diversity. Shall I repeat it, so you have time to get your highlighter pen? YOU CANNOT HAVE UNITY WITHOUT DIVERSITY. Too many marriages have ended because the couples didn't appreciate diversity. What a shame when our Heavenly Father does.

Church, we have a job to do. The Father is waiting to answer His Son's prayer for unity, and we hold the key. It is up to us to lead the way.

CHAPTER 5
RELEASE PEOPLE AND THEIR GIFTS

"You did not choose me, but I chose you and appointed you that you should go and bear fruit and that your fruit should abide, so that whatever you ask the Father in my name, he may give it to you" (John 15:16).

"For as in one body we have many members, and the members do not all have the same function, so we, though many, are one body in Christ, and individually members one of another. Having gifts that differ according to the grace given to us, let us use them: if prophecy in proportion to our faith; if service, in our serving; the one who teaches, in his teaching; the one who exhorts, in his exhortation; the one who contributes, in generosity; the one who leads, with zeal; the one who does acts of mercy, with cheerfulness" (Romans 12:4–8).

Wess Pinkham, a seminary professor at The King's University, said, "When God gives a gift, He wraps it in a person." Agreed. Why, then, do we have so many unopened gifts sitting in the pews on Sunday mornings?

My idea of an unhealthy church is one where the lead pastor does all the work. I describe it as a baby with a big head and a small body. While that's cute at first, it would be disproportionate if it were to continue.

A more significant issue than what it's doing to the pastor and his family, in their physical health and emotional well-being, is what it's **not** doing for the sheep: not allowing them to function in their gifts. In most churches, only 10 percent of the congregants do the work of the ministry. Occasionally, churches that have learned to empower large numbers of volunteers will push that percentage to twenty, but it's rare.

To illustrate, I want you to leave your chair using only 20 percent of your body and walk to the door. Impossible, you say? You're right. Yet, that's what the majority of churches do every week. The pastor does the praying, studying, preaching, and sometimes administrating. At the same time, most people are content to sit, spectate, and often critically judge those involved. Worse, if the pastor falls to infidelity or some such sin, the body is ill-equipped to recover, and another church crumbles.

Pastors who do the lion's share of the work create churches with large heads and small bodies. It was never God's will that one or a few bear the weight of the work. After all, the church is His body, and He is the Head. It is a many-membered body. That is why God has graced all the church members with gifts and the power to function in them.

The Fear Factor

Gifts are easy to recognize in people once you know

what to look for—greeted consistently by friendly smiles? Hospitality. Met an encourager? Probably prophetic. Burns for the mission field? A budding apostle, perhaps. Has patience for people you'd have given up on years prior? That's a pastor in the making. So again, I ask, why do we not recognize and release the gifts in people? Perhaps it's the fear factor. Maybe the pastor fears that if somebody outshines them, they will somehow be less—or worse, out of a job.

This is completely the opposite of Paul's mindset. We can go so far as to say that Paul intended to work himself out of a job. He went from place to place, encouraging believers in their gifts and building them up. The minute God called him elsewhere, he left (Acts 20 is a powerful example).

Paul couldn't have cared less about being outshone by someone. He was faith driven, not fear driven. He also refused to tolerate a spirit of fear in his disciples. After commending Timothy's faith, he says: *"For this reason I remind you fan into flame the gift of God, which is in you through the laying on of my hands, for God has not given us a spirit of fear but of power and love and self-control"* (2 Timothy 1:6–7). Paul repeatedly identified the gifts in people and exhorted them to use them for the kingdom of God.

Furthermore, Paul refused to take credit for anything. Hear his words in 1 Corinthians 3:6–8: *"I planted, Apollos watered, but God gave the growth. So neither he who plants nor he who waters is anything, but only God who gives the growth. He who plants and he who waters are one, and each will receive his wages according to his labor."* The first line in Rick

Warren's book *The Purpose Driven Life* is, "It's not about you." Ultimately, every good and perfect gift is from God (James 1:17) and will be used for His glory. When we reach heaven, we will be thanked as servants, not as lords of the manor (Matthew 25:23). Underutilized gifts in the body of Christ reflect a lord of the manor leadership style. It's time we stop idolizing pastors because they can do it all and begin questioning what motive lies behind it. Maybe that motive is control and fear. If we are not building God's kingdom, we are in dire danger of building our empire.

Empowering the Body

Jesus said He has chosen and appointed you to bring forth fruit that would endure (John 15:16). If Jesus has chosen you, you've also been appointed by Jesus to be productive. A good vineyard owner will constantly inspect the fruit of his field. After all, therein lies his livelihood. What does it benefit him to allow the fruit to rot on the vine? He would be considered the worst owner of all time. As leaders, we best steward the gifts by releasing the body of Christ.

Can you imagine what would happen if everyone in your church understood that they had been deputized, appointed, and anointed by Jesus to turn the world upside down? What if people knew they were as anointed as the preacher, as gifted as the worship leader, as talented as the musicians, as prophetic as the prophet, or as fruitful as the most effective evangelist? Maybe they need someone to tell them that and then release them to function in their giftings.

Professionals with seminary degrees didn't lead the New Testament church. It was led by fishermen, tax collectors, political activists, a doctor, and a self-righteous Pharisee. When he went to Samaria, the first person to start a major revival was a deacon, Philip.

If the church is only built on professionals, it will become mechanical and bureaucratic and lose its sensitivity to the needs of the people. The grassroots level in any organization is the most effective. This couldn't be truer as it relates to the church. What makes the church great is not its more vocal or visible leaders but the rank and file of the ordinary believer, fully engaged.

To quote David and Paul Watson in their book *Contagious Disciple Making*, "By promoting and insisting on a professional clergy, the church has limited its ability and capacity to reach the world for Christ."

This has become a major reason for the massive decline in church attendance and churches in America. We have used only professional clergy to the near exclusion of all others. Even with the addition of Sunday volunteers, it rarely uses more than a small fraction of the total congregation. If we were to throw open the doors of ministry to everyone, all I see is an expansion in every way, numerically, spiritually, and in Christian maturity.

Risk versus Reward

We must understand that people's eternal heavenly rewards hang in the balance. In the parable of the ten talents, gifts buried on earth are wasted (Matthew 25:14–30). Jesus desires for us to have rewards in heaven. Paul, too, was mindful of people's eternal rewards. Even from his prison cell, he thanked the church for financial gifts, assuring them: *"I don't say this because I want a gift from you.*

Rather, I want you to receive a reward for your kindness" (Philippians 4:17 NLT).

Yes, when we release people in their gifts, we do run the risk of people doing it wrong. It was the same in Jesus' day, but He did it anyway; He was mindful of their reward.

We also risk people falling into sin or moral failure, but that already exists in clergy across the denominational spectrum. I argue that we should allow the people to go for it; it can't be worse than what we already have and will likely be hundreds of times more effective. If it gets messy, so what? Revival is messy. As mentioned above, Paul didn't stick around to micromanage the church. He did what he could and left the rest to the Holy Spirit. We would be wise to do the same.

Jesus chose only one qualified leader: Judas Iscariot, the treasurer. Coming from Judea, Judas was the only educated man in the mix; all the others were ordinary, uneducated Galileans (Acts 4:13). Please hear me: it was not the highly educated people who turned the world upside down, but the lower rung of society. Take, for example, the woman at the well. She was so low on the ladder that she had to go to the well alone and in the day's heat. At the end of her time with Jesus, she left and returned with the whole town in tow. Jesus' disciples came back with groceries (John 4).

Paul specifically asks:

Where is the one who is wise? Where is the scribe? Where is the debater of this age? Has not God made foolish the wisdom of the world? For since, in the wisdom of God, the world did not know God through wisdom, it pleased God through the folly of what we preach to save those who believe (1 Corinthians 1:20–21).

He continues in verse 26:

For consider your calling, brothers: not many of you were wise according to worldly standards, not many were powerful, not many were of noble birth. But God chose what is foolish in the world to shame the wise; God chose what is weak in the world to shame the strong. God chose what is low and despised in the world, even things that are not, to bring to nothing things that are.

To look like the body of Christ, we must include people from all walks of life, all shapes, sizes, colors, and abilities, with every member fully engaged and functioning in their calling.

If you hesitate to use people with skills dissimilar to yours, you will remain small in your outreach. You must value diversity and release people precisely because they don't look like you.

The Form of a Servant

Jesus left heaven, took the form of a servant in His time on earth (Philippians 2:6–8), and made Himself nothing. If we consider ourselves servants rather than authoritarian figures, we will more likely recognize and release people in their calling. If we model servanthood, others are more likely to emulate servanthood.

I often ask church leaders if they would rather have a few gifted people leading and preaching on Sundays or hundreds leading and preaching Monday through Saturday. I think I know the answer. It's time to release people in their gifts. Since Jesus has called everybody, we should be doing the same. Since Jesus released His authority to those He called, so should we.

One of the surprising results of releasing people to function in their gifts is that it takes the load off you. What made Kingdom Global Ministries, the ministry Devi and I led, different from other ministries is that we did not hire people for what they could do for us but for what we could do for them. I wanted our ministry to be a point of discovery and release; you discover your greatest gifts, and Kingdom Global will walk with you as you come into the fullness of your calling.

In September 2018, Felipe Hasegawa, our incredible assistant of nine years, resigned. One of the great gifts of Felipe, among his many, was his skill in interpretation. He interpreted hundreds of sermons for us in Portuguese as we traveled throughout Brazil. When he resigned, he left a large hole to fill.

Shortly after his resignation, the Holy Spirit prompted me to call John Marques. I had known John as a Fall River, Massachusetts, worship leader for many years. I didn't know, or at least hadn't remembered, that John's family was from the Azores, an autonomous region of Portugal in the mid-Atlantic, and he spoke fluent Portuguese, as did his wife, Dory. I was aware of neither John's brilliance in technical information, skill as a sound engineer, giftedness in dealing with businesspeople, knowledge of financial spreadsheets, his power as a worship leader, nor his tremendous pastoral heart. I discovered all these gifts, which were invaluable to us, while working with him.

Recently, Gateway, a megachurch in the DFW area,

brought John on staff, significantly increasing his benefits, influence, and pastoral responsibilities among their dozens of worship leaders. I would love to take credit for John's release. Unfortunately, I can't. It was all the Holy Spirit. But I can rejoice that God used me and others in his life to identify one of those popularly called "laity" and open new doors of opportunity for him in the body of Christ.

Those "others" in John's life were people like his Uncle Gabe. Gabe was John's first pastor at Champions for Christ in Dartmouth, Massachusetts. He called John, a construction worker then, from the pews and into his ultimate calling. John's mom and dad were also releasers. They released their sons, John and Samson, to flourish. Now John continues the legacy by releasing his children into their calling, and both are exceptional.

Let's move away from the term laity. If Jesus chose you, He anointed and appointed you. We are all preachers of the gospel in some way. Some preach behind a pulpit, others in classrooms, kitchens, offices, government, or construction worksites, but everyone has a pulpit.

Professional Clergy

It is destructive for the professional clergy to dominate the people of Jesus Christ's church. When Emperor Constantine declared Christianity the state religion, he combined it with pagan practices. Thus began the concept of the clergy as an elite group of religious professionals separated from and ruling over the "subservient, unqualified laity." Nothing has been more injurious to the growth of the church.

In Revelation 2:1 – 7, Jesus addresses the church in

Ephesus. In his address, He commends the Ephesians for hating the work of the Nicolaitans. Although I cannot prove it, I believe the doctrine of the Nicolaitans, described in Revelation 2:6 (and also in Revelation 2:15), talks about a practice of conquering the laity rather than speaking of a person named Nicolas, per se. Church history often points to one of the first deacons in the early church, the proselyte Nicolas, as the one to whom Jesus was referring, but this cannot be proven.

The word Nicolaitan comprises two Greek words, *nikos*, meaning *victory* or *overcoming*, and *laos*, meaning *people*. Combined, the words together mean to conquer the laity. Whether I'm right or wrong is irrelevant. The point is that the church in Ephesus didn't like what the Nicolaitans were doing, nor did Jesus. If my theory is correct, it will do us well to have the same attitude: Jesus doesn't want anyone dominating His church, most of all, professional clergy. We are all, whether professionally trained or novices in the faith, to be ministers of the gospel, making no distinction between the higher-ups or the "lower-downs."

The Wiki Church

An incredible example of lay people's ability to produce results quickly can be seen in the history of Wikipedia, the people's encyclopedia. Though there was a prior version of Wikipedia before January 2001, something changed that took it from a small, struggling company to one of the largest and most powerful in the world. What was the change?

The earlier version of Wikipedia was called Nupedia. Only professionals were allowed to write and edit articles.

Things exploded after January 15, 2001, when the leaders used ordinary people rather than professionals. The first thing they discovered was that the accuracy of the content was the same. The nonprofessionals were as accurate as the professionals. Secondly, lay contributors took a shorter time to produce the finished article.

I was exposed to this concept of lay leadership, not through the study of the history of Wikipedia but by reading Steve Murrell's book, *The Wiki Church*. I have believed in the power of lay leadership for years but had never heard it articulated before.

Steve Murrell says, "It took the experts three years to create twenty-four articles and the nonexperts one year to create twenty thousand articles." Within a few years, there were hundreds of thousands of new articles. What earlier took months and years now takes days and months. Articles proliferated, and readership skyrocketed. Today the readership of Wikipedia has over fifteen billion page views. "Wiki" came from the Hawaiian word, *wiki*, meaning quick or fast. Imagine how quickly the church would grow if we released the "wiki" lane, the nonprofessional leaders in our churches?

Using the principle of release, Steve Murrell built Victory Church in Manilla from 165 university students to over fifty-three thousand members. All this while church attendance in the Philippines was declining. To quote Steve, "Jesus told His followers that He would build His church, and then He told them to go and make disciples. It's that simple. We make disciples, and He builds the church." I couldn't agree more.

This does not diminish the need for seminary or Bible-college-trained leaders in our churches. Instead, it releases ordinary men and women to do the work of the ministry as well.

Release God's People

In my previous pastorates, I preached, "Don't bring people to church to get them saved. You lead them to the Lord out in the marketplace. You baptize them in water, lay hands on them, pray over them to receive the Holy Spirit, teach them the Word and disciple them, then bring them to the church building to meet me and the rest of their family." I even encouraged them to serve communion in their homes, something entirely scriptural.

In life, there are two kinds of people, controllers, and releasers. I choose to be the latter. In my early ministry, I was a controller. I thought that to be a good "head," I had to control every detail of the church. I even boasted that I rarely took vacations. I was convinced God wouldn't move and revival wouldn't come unless I did everything (or at least controlled it). Since then, I've learned that the reward of leadership is when you release people, not when you control them.

If you have a thousand members in your congregation, you should see them as a thousand preachers in your church, each recognized and released by you. There could be no greater honor than to see those you lead released in their skills and anointing to do the work of the ministry. Our goal should be to see every member of the body of Christ fully functioning in their gifts and building eternal rewards.

CHAPTER 6
BECOME A SERVANT

"…though he was in the form of God, did not count equality with God a thing to be grasped, made himself nothing, taking the form of a servant, being born in the likeness of men" (Philippians 2:6–7).

"Let the greatest among you become as the youngest, and the leader as one who serves. For who is the greater, one who reclines at table or one who serves? Is it not the one who reclines at table? But I am among you as the one who serves" (Luke 22:26–27).

Before one of my lectures at a Bible training school in Dallas, Texas, a student asked me what position I filled in the body of Christ. "Are you an apostle, prophet, evangelist, pastor, or teacher?"

"Servant," I responded. The look on his face indicated he wasn't satisfied with my answer.

"No, *really*, what are you?"

"I'm *really* just a servant," I repeated. Nothing is more

dissatisfying to people than an answer they didn't anticipate.

Wouldn't it save a lot of stationery, desk nameplates, church marquees, business cards, reserved parking-spot signs, and biographical sketches, not to mention bloviated bombastic self-promotion, if everyone was just a servant? It would also save many egos from arising to positions of pride God didn't intend. And should, God forbid, one of our leaders fall, it's a much shorter distance to fall if we are all just servants and not in elevated positions of power and prominence. The higher you are on the ladder of success, the greater the fall when you fail.

Resisted versus Assisted

The reward of a servant is also much better because God chooses the lowly before the haughty; He exalts the humble. As Jesus' mother, Mary, declared in her song of praise, *"My soul magnifies the Lord…for he has looked on the humble estate of his servant."* As she continues to exalt God and His dethroning of the proud, she says, *"He has brought down the mighty from their thrones and exalted those of humble estate"* (Luke 1:46–48, 52).

I look at it this way; you can either be assisted by God in your ministry or resisted by Him. In a world fraught with anxiety, 1 Peter 5:5–7 holds the key. Before you cast your anxieties on God, clothe yourself in humility, for *"God opposes the proud but gives grace to the humble."* Check yourself. Are you anxious? Meeting resistance in your relationships and ministry? It's possible you need to humble yourself.

No Greater Calling

God makes the least in the kingdom the greatest. I rather doubt we will see big titles in heaven. If Jesus called John the Baptist the least in the kingdom of God, I think it behooves us to seek the lower position so God can bid us to come higher on graduation day (Matthew 11:11, Luke 14:10).

The heart of a servant is not just for leaders but for every believer. At the Last Supper, when Jesus cloaked Himself with the servant's towel, He intended to show every disciple that the lower one gets in this life, the higher he gets in God's kingdom.

Servants had no rights. Neither do we. We don't even have the right to be right. We lost our rights and everything else when we came to Jesus. We are dead, and our life is hidden in Christ (Colossians 3:1–11). We live in Him and through Him. If Jesus came as a servant, that is our calling as well. There is no greater title in this world than to be a servant of Jesus Christ. We are bond servants, having been purchased from the slave block of our sins by the blood of Jesus Christ.

During the blight of slavery in American history, the slave owner should have known this truth; the enslaved person was greater than the master. Had they reversed the roles, they might have seen Jesus in the flesh because He looked just like the slaves and servants. They missed the greatest opportunity in history to liberate and then serve those who had been enslaved.

Change Your Title to Servant Before It's Too Late

Again, if you must give yourself a title, make it

"servant." As a reference, I'll identify some Old Testament figures called servants: Abraham, Isaac, Jacob, Joshua, Moses, David, Isaiah, and the pagan king of Babylon, Nebuchadnezzar. But my all-time favorite servant reference is Job when God volunteered him to be tested by the devil. *"Have you ever considered my servant Job?"* (Job 1:8). With friends like that, who needs enemies? Notice that when God volunteered someone He thought could sustain the trials and come out on the other end unscathed, He turned to His *servant*, Job. That's a powerful key.

An interesting story occurs in the New Testament where a demon-possessed girl trailed Paul and Silas for many days, repeatedly crying out, *"These are servants of the Most High God, who proclaim to you the way of salvation."* Finally, Paul had enough. *"I command you in the name of Jesus Christ to come out of her"* (Acts 16:17–18). Even demons can spot a true leader; one in the guise of a servant.

To gain an appreciation for the attitude and humility of the apostles, most of the writers of the New Testament epistles entitled themselves *"(Name)_____ a servant of Jesus Christ."* If their leader, Jesus Christ, considered Himself a servant, how could they do less? Occasionally Paul added the descriptive moniker "prisoner," equally humbling. Even James, the half brother of Jesus, called himself a servant (James 1:1).

I don't want to get to heaven and discover I've given myself a title higher than the one Jesus took, do you?

John the Beloved begins the book of Revelation with the words, *"The revelation of Jesus Christ, which God gave him to show to his **servants** the things that must soon take place."* He continues, *"He made it known by sending his angel to his servant John"* (Revelation 1:1, emphasis added). Interestingly, the longest apocalyptic book in the Bible is written by a **servant** and addressed to **servants**.

Jesus the Servant

Jesus is identified as the servant of God in both the Old and New Testaments. In Zechariah 3:8, Jesus is prophetically called "my **servant** the Branch."

In Isaiah 42:1, the prophet called the coming messiah, *"Behold my **servant**, whom I uphold, my chosen, in whom my soul delights."* The prophecy is fulfilled in Matthew 12:18–22 and refers to Jesus.

Isaiah 53:11 also identifies Jesus as the Suffering **Servant**: *"Out of the anguish of his soul he shall see and be satisfied; by his knowledge shall the righteous one, my **servant**, make many to be accounted righteous, and he shall bear their iniquities."*

In Acts 4:30, the early church prayed for healing, signs, and wonders *"through the name of your holy **servant** Jesus."*

Bottom of the Barrel

When I look for potential leaders, I don't look for the most outgoing personalities or aggressive leadership styles; I look for those who know how to serve. When the event is over, they stay and help to clean up without being asked. When you need something done, you can always count on them. They come early and leave late.

Food items used to be sold in barrels. An idiom based on this describes whether someone is worthy of an important role. If they're worthy, they're considered top of the barrel. If not, they're the crushed leftovers at the bottom of the barrel. Be like Jesus and elevate the lowly. Scrape the barrel; seek the ones humble enough to serve.

One man told me, "When you get the bandwagon moving, tell me, and I'll jump on."

What arrogance.

I responded, "When I get the bandwagon moving, I won't need you." He wanted to wait until all the work was done before joining in. I can't think of a spirit more opposite that of Jesus, who came to this earth as a servant.

Servants get little recognition, are on the bottom of the social ladder, have no promise of a future, cannot aspire for greatness, are not rewarded for their labor, and are always under someone else's authority. Freedom is not a dream; it's an impossibility.

Though I can't locate the source, I've heard many comment that if serving is beneath you, leading is above you.

In 1 Corinthians 4:1, Paul says, *"This is how one should regard us, as **servants** of Christ and stewards of the mysteries of God."* The word used here for *servants* in Greek is *huperetes*. It comprises two words, *huper,* meaning *under,* and *eresso,* meaning *to row*. It referred to the bottom rowers of the three-banked Roman and Greek war galleys called *triremes*.

As a *huperetes*, you would never see the light of day. You'd be on the bottom of the boat, rowing day and night. No wonder we don't have too many volunteers. Who wants to work without being noticed or labor with no reward?

"Hey, let's give a hand to that guy on the bottom of the trireme. Have you ever seen a better bottom rower? Look at him sweat."

Yet that is who Paul says we are. We are just under-rowers. No Olympic medals, no Super Bowl rings, no signed certificates of excellence, no applause, and no recognition, at least in this life. But in eternity, we will hear the Lord's commendation, *"Well gone, good and faithful servant"* (Matthew 25:21,23).

Gabriel Zamora is the young man who replaced me this year as President of Kingdom Global Ministries, the nonprofit mission organization my wife, Devi, and I founded over thirty years ago. I've observed his leadership skills for over a decade. I've witnessed youth by the thousands respond to his call to give everything they have and follow Jesus. I've seen how he and his wife, Domonique, train their three children to be godly, respectful, and well-behaved. And his delivery of the Word of God is eloquent, exceptional, masterful, and anointed.

But what impressed me most was watching him after a Teleios Men's gathering. After all the men departed, he and Domonique refused to leave the meeting room until every chair had been returned to its place and every piece of litter, empty water bottle, and can were picked up. They moved toward the door only after everything was organized and prepared for the next day. Even my prodding to get them to go home and put their family to bed was useless. They wouldn't budge. That's all I needed to show me what great leaders they are.

I fear we are raising a generation of leaders who, in search of significance or notoriety, prefer to go from the pew to the pulpit, bypassing the serving process. Their only examples are the high-profile preachers with an entourage of hirelings and lackeys who attend to their ever-more-privileged demands. They have never witnessed the leader washing the feet of others. Of course, those leaders are there, but not as visible, their work concealed by an "others first" approach.

At my wife's, Devi's, memorial service, one of the eulogists described her experience with Devi at the first Home Experience Intensive in Youngstown, Ohio. Joan Evrist is a pastor's wife from Nashville, Tennessee, and spoke these words:

I was at the first Home Experience at the Mentoring Mansion in Ohio. I will never forget how hard she [Devi] worked to prepare things for that first weekend. The air-conditioning wasn't working, and it was hot! She was quite sweaty (or, as she would say—glowing), and yet she continued like the warrior she was. And that first night, after working so hard all week, she showed up at my room around 10:00 p.m., ready to give me a foot massage! I was shocked! I said, "I should be massaging your feet!"

She replied, "After I massage your and your roommates' feet, you can massage mine!" We stayed up late and had a blast!

She modeled servanthood and servant leadership. After leaving that weekend, my life was forever changed! Which meant the lives of all those I was connected to were about to change.

The pattern Devi set at that first Intensive, when on the opening night she washed and massaged the feet of every woman who came to the Mentoring Mansion, continued throughout the years. Over the next twenty years, she washed and massaged the feet of over fourteen hundred women. To be precise, that amounts to two thousand eight hundred feet. She did all this after she set the table, cooked their dinner, and taught them for two hours. I'm tired just thinking about it.

Several years later, my daughter Trina had an encounter with the Lord in a dream. He told her that she would spend the next season of her life serving her mom. Only the Holy Spirit could have known that Trina would take Devi's mantle and ministry after Devi's passing and spread it to the world.

Trina was already the ultimate servant. I have never seen anyone who served so many people. Her seven-bedroom home operated like a hotel filled continually with people who needed help, encouragement, counseling, or protection day in and day out. But this call was different. Her assignment now was to serve her mother.

In the final years of her life, Trina served Devi continually. On December 28, 2022, Devi passed to her heavenly reward, and her baton was handed to Trina, and the dream became a reality. Since then, God has opened doors in multiple nations and states to Trina. Hundreds of women have volunteered and continue to volunteer desiring to partner with Devi and Trina's vision to restore the dignity and sanctity of the home. When God needed someone to carry on the legacy of Devi, He needed to look no further than to the one who had been serving her for years.

When you are looking for someone to replace you, you might want to look behind you for those who have faithfully served you in the past.

A Yes and No Process

The only valid path to promotion is through the door of faithful service. Any other route is self-promotional and will lead to eventual failure.

The truly great leaders I've followed are those who had years or decades of unseen service to others until God opened the door to their ultimate calling. Like Joseph in the Old Testament, I can only imagine how many times they longed to be out of the prison cell of serving others and breathing the pure oxygen of their leadership initiative. Will that day ever come? Will I have my own leadership position someday? Will I have my own ministry? Will there be a time when I can practice what I've learned?

In one way, yes, and in another, no.

On the one hand, no. If you've studied the life of Joseph, you will note that even though he was second in command only to Pharoah, he remained submitted and in servitude to him his whole life (Genesis 46). Those of us who have chosen to be leaders in the body of Christ will always be servants, no matter how lofty our title, position, or salary. If Christ chose to make serving a life calling, so can we. Serving will never be beneath us. And it will never lose its reward of blessing others.

On the other hand, yes. Serving is not the end-all, but the process whereby God produces character in us, prunes the ever-preening ego, and releases us into our true anointing. So, serving is both a consistent, daily inner heart attitude as well as the door to future success and ultimate fulfillment.

This is aptly illustrated in some of the last words of

Jesus in the parable of the talents in Matthew 25. Twice He responded to the investors who had multiplied their talents with the words, *"Well done, good and faithful servant."* In verse 21, He said to one, *"You have been faithful over a little; I will set you over much."* And to the other, in verse 23, He gave the same reward to set him over much but added the additional blessing, *"Enter into the joy of your Master."* I'm hard pressed to know which is the greater reward. I would choose the latter; simply seeing the joy on Jesus' face when we bow before Him with the harvest is reward enough. Yet Jesus always pays His servants; it's just a matter of time.

In Luke 19, a similar story is told but with different metrics. Ten servants are given ten minas. A mina is a Greek measurement of a worker's three-month wages. Their reward was much more defined: one was given ten cities, and the other five. That is an incredible reward for serving just a matter of months. God is not stingy in paying His servants.

I would be remiss if I didn't also mention the punishment reserved for the slothful servant. Not only was his mina taken away from him and given to the one who had ten, but he was slaughtered along with all those who refused to be ruled over by their master. My mind cannot comprehend the severity meted out to those who refuse to serve the Master who died for them.

An Expression of Love

Before closing this chapter, I want to mention one more major outcome of serving. Serving is the penultimate (versus ultimate) expression of love. I say penultimate for a reason. Expressing love has many facets, as expressed by

Paul in 1 Corinthians 13, where he describes what love is and what love does: it is patient and kind, does not envy or boast, is not arrogant or rude, and doesn't insist on having its way.

Jesus is more specific. According to His teaching, the ultimate expression of love is when one lays down his life for his friend (John 15:13). Therefore, I call serving the penultimate expression of love. It's next in line. One doesn't die physically when he serves others, but he does die to self.

I cannot say I truly love someone if I'm unwilling to serve them. I believe this so strongly.

Don't tell me you love your spouse, family, or peers if you're unwilling to serve them.

In that context, serving is inextricably connected to true love. No serving, no love. No matter how often you tell your spouse or family you love them, your love language is difficult to prove if you don't serve them. You're part of the noisy clang of percussion instruments Paul refers to in 1 Corinthians 13:1; your words are merely vacuous noise and void of authenticity.

In the years of Devi's battle with cancer, I found my greatest calling in life: to leave all and serve my wife. After all, at the onset of cancer, she had faithfully served me for over fifty-six years; how could I do any less? But to me, it was the opposite of laborious. Without exaggeration, I loved every minute I served her. Serving never became servile or resented.

People would often ask me, "How are you doing?"

My response was always the same, "I thoroughly enjoy serving my wife and making it my life's work." She was my ministry. Everything else was laid aside. For twenty-four hours a day, I served her. Day and night, I responded to the smallest request:

Honey, I'm cold. Do you mind bringing me another blanket?

Honey, I'm so thirsty. I hate you getting up, but I need some water.

I don't want to bother you, but do you mind bringing me a pain pill?

Bother me, are you kidding? It was my greatest pleasure in life. Jesus said, in Matthew 25, when we do it to others, we do it to Him. Though He was unseen, in the years of serving Devi, I was also serving Jesus.

At the time of this writing, it is three months since her passing. I have recalled the thousands of times we said, "I love you" to each other. But all the verbalized "I love you" could never be validated unless we had served each other. Unless love includes serving, it will never have the ring of authenticity or sincerity.

I don't need to list all the areas of serving that consumed my last several years. I do not need self-righteous accolades. They are hollow anyway. After all, I was only doing what Jesus would expect me to do. I was motivated by love. But I will mention a few that might spark a response in you, my reader, and open new ideas of how you can better serve your spouse.

- I heated the car for her in advance so she wouldn't be chilled when she got in.
- I served her breakfast in bed on multiple occasions.

- I sat beside her bed every night as we enjoyed conversation, a movie, or a documentary together.
- I always opened the door for her, whether car, home, or restaurant.
- I made her schedule my priority. Everything revolved around her medical needs and appointments.
- I did the grocery shopping.
- I took her to hundreds of doctor appointments and waited in her room during infusions.
- I spent hours praying for her.
- I protected her when people innocently wore her down through lengthy one-way conversations. As diplomatically as possible, I would say, "Honey, you look like you're getting tired. Do you need to take a nap?" Hint: Visitor, go home!
- I held her hand through the night.
- I massaged her neck, back, arms, and legs.
- I got up in the middle of the night to get her pain medications.
- I made the bed every day.
- I did the washing.
- I often drove her around because she was too sick to go to a mall or restaurant but too bored to stay home.

My reward was in the serving itself. And so, I say again, no matter how much you love your spouse, children, church, and friends, if it doesn't include serving, I don't think it qualifies to be called love. Simply said, love prefers the other person (Romans 12:10). There's a challenging illustration given by Jesus in Luke 17:7–10 that perfectly illustrates the attitude we are to embrace as servants:

Will any one of you who has a servant plowing or keeping sheep say to him when he has come in from the field, "Come at once and recline at table"? Will he not rather say to him, "Prepare supper for me, and dress properly, and serve me while I eat and drink, and afterward you will eat and drink"? Does he thank the servant because he did what was commanded? So you also, when you have done all that you were commanded, say, "We are unworthy servants; we have only done what was our duty."

It doesn't matter how great a minister you think you are; it's time to don the apron and towel, fill up the basin and begin serving. You will never be greater than your commitment to serving. Love serves. I'll see you with the rest of the rowers at the bottom. Can I hear an Amen?

CHAPTER 7
PRAY AT ALL TIMES

"All these with one accord were devoting themselves to prayer, together with the women and Mary the mother of Jesus, and his brothers" (Acts 1:14).

"...praying at all times in the Spirit, with all prayer and supplication" (Ephesians 6:18).

God designed our lives to be one of unending communion with Him. Genesis 2:7 says, *"Then the LORD God formed the man of dust from the ground and breathed into his nostrils the breath of life, and the man became a living creature."* The first face Adam saw when he opened his eyes was the LORD God. A careful reading of Genesis 1 and 2 reveals how often they communicated.

- God spoke a blessing of rule and fruitfulness over Adam and Eve (Genesis 1:28).
- God talked to Adam and Eve about His abundant provision for them (Genesis 1:29–30).

- God warned Adam not to eat the fruit on the Tree of the Knowledge of Good and Evil (Genesis 2:17).
- Adam named the animals with God (Genesis 2:19).
- God taught Adam how to keep the garden (Genesis 2:15).

Adam and Eve talked about everything with God until the fateful day they decided not to. In complete rebellion, they believed the serpent's lie, disregarded God's commands, ate from the Tree of the Knowledge of Good and Evil, and ushered sin and death into Paradise. God called to His children in the cool of the evening, but for the first time, they hid from His presence in shame (Genesis 3:8–9).

Adam and Eve had *every* answer to *every* question or need they could imagine right next to them in the person of God (Genesis 3:8), but it wasn't enough for them. Proverbs 2:6 says, *"For the LORD gives wisdom; from his mouth come knowledge and understanding."* God is the source of wisdom and knowledge, and we cannot circumvent our relationship with Him to obtain it through any other means, no matter how appealing that forbidden fruit is. We are God's creation, and He is the Creator. We cannot do a single thing apart from Him. When we try, everything falls apart.

The Prayerful Son

As the perfect Son, Jesus utterly rejected the notion of doing anything on His own. He said, *"Truly, truly, I say to you, the Son can do nothing of his own accord, but only what he sees the Father doing. For whatever the Father does, that the Son does likewise"* (John 5:19). Jesus restored everything Adam and Eve relinquished, including a lifestyle of unbroken communion and communication with Father God. Jesus talked to God constantly and modeled the humility of a prayerful life to His disciples. Every step He took was in submission to the will of God, His Father.

However, during the three and a half years His disciples followed Jesus of Nazareth, there is no recorded instance where *they* prayed. A careful reading of the Gospels indicates that every time Jesus prayed all night, the disciples were asleep, including during His multiple prayers in the garden. Finding Peter asleep, Jesus' final question remains unanswered, *"So, could you not watch* [stay awake] *with me one hour?"* (Matthew 26:40). I think we know the answer, No!

Even though the disciples asked Jesus how to pray in Matthew 6:9–13, they evidently didn't practice prayer. I've yet to find a single Scripture where they prayed. But every time they looked for Jesus, they found Him praying, whether in the wilderness, on the mountaintop, or in the presence of others.

In Mark 9:28, the disciples asked Jesus why He could cast out demons, and they couldn't. In verse 29, His response is classic: I pray, and you don't. (My version.)

Mark 1:35 shows what appears to be the routine of Jesus. *"And rising very early in the morning, while it was still dark, he departed and went out to a desolate place, and there he prayed."* Luke 4:42 references the same event but doesn't specifically say He prayed. However, chronologically it is the same event.

Eight References to Jesus' Prayer Life in Luke:

Luke's gospel records the most instances of Jesus praying:

One:

In Luke 3:21, the heavens opened, God spoke, and the Holy Spirit descended upon Jesus as He prayed.

Two:

In Luke 5:16, the extended, early morning prayer of Jesus resulted in the power of the Holy Spirit healing the paralyzed man who was lowered from the ceiling.

Three:

In Luke 6:12, Jesus went up to the mountain to pray, and after praying all night, selected the twelve disciples.

This passage highlighted an incongruency between my ministry and that of Jesus. I have selected dozens of leaders without a single prayer being uttered. My negligence resulted in dozens of failures created by me and my lack of prayer. I find no solace that I'm not the only leader who has made major decisions without consulting the Lord or the Holy Spirit. What could the outcome have been had I waited in prayer until the Lord revealed His will on which leaders to appoint and release? What tragic consequences could have been avoided had I spent time with the Lord before making rash decisions? I know this prayerlessness was the norm rather than the exception for me. God forgive me.

After the all-night prayer meeting in Luke 6:12, not only were the disciples selected, but a multitude of people were healed of their diseases. People even tried to touch Jesus because the power of the Holy Spirit was emanating from Him and healing them all. We may need more all-night prayer meetings.

Four:

In Luke 11 and 18, Jesus gives two parables related to prayer. In Luke 11, Jesus describes a presumptuous man awakening his sleeping friend to plead for three loaves of bread to feed another presumptuous friend. Because of his insistence, and impudence, the door finally opened, and the bread was distributed.

That becomes the illustration Jesus uses to introduce the subject of persistence in prayer. *"Ask and it will be given to you, seek, and you will find; knock, and it will be opened to you. For everyone who asks receives, and the one who seeks finds, and to the one who knocks it will be opened"* (Luke 11:9–10).

That Scripture alone should expand our knowledge about the purpose and power of prayer. But Jesus isn't finished until He introduces the Father into the equation.

"What father among you, if his son asks for a fish, will instead of a fish give him a serpent; or if he asks for an egg, will give him a scorpion? If you then, who are evil, know how to give good gifts to your children, how much more will the heavenly Father give the Holy Spirit to those who ask him!" (Luke 11:11–13).

Notice how the request for bread opens a whole new subject, the Father's willingness to extravagantly bless His children with gifts, including the precious gift of the Holy Spirit. Now, that's a big gift and a big answer to prayer.

Five:

The second significant chapter on prayer is in Luke 18. In this chapter, a parable introduces a godless judge and an annoying widow who wouldn't be quiet until her need for justice was satisfied. Her insistence on being given justice wore the judge down. He couldn't take it anymore.

Jesus' explanation of the parable was priceless: *"And will not God give justice to his elect, who cry to him day and night? Will he delay long over them? I tell you, he will give justice to them speedily"* (Luke 18:7). Then He adds a caveat as a warning: *"Nevertheless, when the Son of Man comes, will he find faith on earth?"* (Luke 18:8). There must be a connection between persistent prayer, *"...who cry to him day and night,"* and faith. Faith, like prayer, never gives up.

Six:

In Luke 9:18, he says, *"Now it happened that as he was praying alone, the disciples were with him."* That is, Jesus was the one praying, not the disciples. Luke goes on to record the fact that it was this prayer of Jesus that elicited Peter's famous response, *"[You are] The Christ of God"* (v. 20) or, as Matthew states, who also records this instance but not in the context of Jesus' prayer, *"You are the Christ, the Son of the living God"* (Matthew 16:16).

This is such a great illustration of how each gospel reveals another facet of the incomparable life of Jesus Christ. I'm so glad we have this additional information. It confirms the importance of prayer in the life of Christ and the revelation His prayer provoked within Peter.

Seven:

Luke 9:28–36 records the transfiguration of Jesus.

"And as he was praying, the appearance of his face was altered, and his clothing became dazzling white. And behold, two men were talking with him, Moses and Elijah, who appeared in glory and spoke of his departure [exodus] which he was about to accomplish in Jerusalem" (Luke 9:29–31).

Guess what the disciples were doing? You guessed it, sleeping. But let's concentrate on all that happened as a result of Jesus' prayer:

- His countenance was changed.
- His clothing became luminescent.
- Moses and Elijah also appeared with Him in glory, discussing His future departure from this world.
- The disciples, upon awakening, saw His glory.
- God the Father spoke to Him from heaven.

Not bad for one prayer session, albeit a lengthy one.

Eight:

In Luke 22, Jesus bids the disciples to stay awake with Him for at least one hour while He prays. Since He prayed three times on this occasion, presumably, His request that they stay awake for an hour was a minimal appeal. However, their flesh won out, and He prayed alone.

The gospel of Luke is the only one that records the intensity of Jesus' Gethsemane prayer. It makes sense that Luke, the physician, would record that the capillaries burst in His body, turning His sweat into blood.

The fervency of Jesus' prayer life is expressed in poignant detail in Hebrews, along with why His prayers were heard. *"In the days of his flesh, Jesus offered up prayers and supplications, with loud cries and tears, to him who was able to save him from death, and he was heard because of his reverence"* (Hebrews 5:7). Note that though He was heard, He was not spared a torturous death. But as the obedient Son, He fully complied with the Father. His final prayers were for others: God's will, not His, and for His disciples. In John 17, which scholars call the High Priestly Prayer of Jesus, the major topic of His final intercession is for His disciples. I can't think of anything more selfless than Jesus spending His last hours praying for the eleven, fully knowing they would soon deny Him.

Prayer Birthing the Miraculous

When Jesus walked on the water, it directly resulted from prayer. In Matthew 14:23, after Jesus had dispersed the crowd, He immediately went up to the top of the mountain to pray and spend the night in prayer. *"When evening came, he was there alone"* indicates He arrived at the top of the mountain before sunset. Another time frame is mentioned in verse 25. *"And in the fourth watch of the night."* The fourth watch, according to Roman time, would have been from 3 to 6 a.m. Sometime between 3 and 6 a.m., after having spent the night in prayer, Jesus is seen walking on water.

How many miracles have occurred due to concerted evenings spent in prayer? Only God knows.

On my numerous trips to Africa, I've noticed how committed the churches are to praying. In thousands of churches, one Friday a month, the saints pray through the entire night. A prayer meeting in one Lagos, Nigeria, church garners up to a million people praying throughout the night. I can confirm the existence of these massive prayer meetings because, on multiple occasions, my hotel was adjacent to their gatherings. Unlike the disciples, I rarely went to sleep; their ear-splitting sound systems kept me awake nearly the entire night. It shows how unspiritual I am. I hoped they would quit praying and go to bed so I could sleep.

There has been a massive global emphasis on prayer in recent years, with entire internet networks devoting twenty-four hours daily to prayer. Prayer rooms are common in hundreds of churches and nearly every nation. People are praying, and God is moving.

The Prayers of the Saints

In my opinion, global revival will not occur without the prayers of the saints. In addition, I'm convinced, according to Revelation 5:8 and 8:3, that these prayers trigger end-time events. Notice in each instance when the prayer vials are emptied, something cataclysmic occurs:

In Revelation 5:8, as the prayer vials are poured forth, the Lamb of God breaks the seals and opens the scrolls, beginning the events of the Great Tribulation.

In Revelation 8:3, the angel collects the prayers of the saints in a golden censer (bowl) from the golden altar. When combined with fire, it erupts with peals of thunder, rumblings, flashes of lightning, and earthquakes. In verse 6, the seven angels begin blowing their trumpets, portending the end of this age and the beginning of the kingdom of God.

I would suggest that your prayers are more powerful than you can ever imagine. Need I tell you, contrary to the devil's lies, your prayers are efficacious? God has chosen two primary tools for the believer to partner with Him. One is worship, and the other is prayer.

It's also interesting to note that of all the defensive armaments Paul introduces in Ephesians 6, the only offensive weapons are the Word of God and prayer. *"And take the helmet of salvation, and the sword of the Spirit, which is the Word of God, praying at all times in the Spirit, with all prayer and supplication"* (Ephesians 6:17–18).

The remainder of the New Testament is replete with examples of prayer and the answers to prayer.

The Book of Acts

Acts chronicles several instances of concerted prayer. The pattern is set in Acts 1:14, where the disciples continually devoted themselves to prayer. It's nice to know that the disciples, who slept through every prayer meeting while Jesus was on earth, now replicated the pattern of their Master.

Notice how common prayer was in the book of Acts. Except for chapter 15 (which I will discuss), every chapter, from 1 to 16, contains a reference to prayer. Though chapter 5 doesn't record the specific occasion of prayer, it does record that it took place at Solomon's Porch, the early church's place of prayer.

Chapter 1:

The church prayed continually.

Chapter 2:

I'm convinced the 10-day waiting in the Upper Room was more than just a time of fellowship or potluck meals, but prayerful waiting on the Holy Spirit's arrival on the Day of Pentecost. This is confirmed in verse 42, which says the disciples devoted themselves to prayer.

Chapter 3:

The disciples are on their way to Solomon's Porch, the place of prayer, when the lame man is healed.

Chapter 4:

The church prays fervently for God to extend his hand to heal and perform signs and wonders when the house begins to shake violently under the power of an earthquake, an obvious confirmation of their prayer being heard.

Chapter 5:

While this chapter doesn't specifically say that the Church prayed, it does state that signs, wonders, and miracles were done by the hands of the Apostles, which throughout scripture is always preceded by prayer. And it took place at Solomon's Porch, the place of prayer.

Chapter 6:

The deacons are chosen through the laying on of hands and prayer.

Chapter 7:

Stephen prays as his spirit is received into heaven.

Chapter 8:

James and John arrive from Jerusalem to pray for the new Samaritan believers to receive the Holy Spirit.

Chapter 9:

Ananias is instructed to go to Straight Street and minister to Saul of Tarsus, who will be praying.

Chapter 10:

The Gentile world is brought into the knowledge of Jesus and the kingdom of God through the prayers of Cornelius.

Chapter 11:

The report of Cornelius' prayer is given to the church in Jerusalem.

Chapter 12

While the church prays, Peter is delivered from prison.

Chapter 13:

The prophets and teachers lay hands on Barnabas and Paul, pray, and send them out on the first apostolic mission of the early church.

Chapter 14:

The first missionary church elders are appointed and anointed through prayer and fasting.

Chapter 15:

Curiously, the only time the church didn't pray was in Acts 15, at their congregational (denominational) meeting. It seems like that should be where prayer is most needed when apostles, elders, and congregations assemble. How can anything of value be accomplished without consulting heaven first?

The Bible tells us that there was much debate (Acts 15:7) at the meeting, so we can only imagine it was fraught with tension and varying opinions. Although they found unity, it is noteworthy that a "sharp disagreement" (Acts 15:39) arose right after the council between Saul and Barnabus over John Mark. Could this have been avoided by an atmosphere bathed in prayer? We will never know.

Chapter 16:

As soon as Paul arrives at his Macedonian assignment, he immediately goes to the river, a place of prayer. After his arrest, Paul and Silas begin their prayer and praise meeting at midnight, leading the jailer and his household to salvation.

Unasked Prayers

In James 4:2, the Lord's half-brother suggests you have not because you ask not, meaning if you don't pray about it, you go without.

I have often wondered how many prayers God would answer if we only asked. As for me, I want to ask as often (and as big) as possible while still on this earth. I want my prayers to fill God's heavenly storehouse. I don't want to arrive in heaven and find God had so much more in store if only I'd asked.

At a midweek service in our first pastorate in Washington State, a teenage girl asked to share a dream she'd had. I was only too happy to hand her the microphone. In her dream, an angelic guide showed her the wonders of heaven. Suddenly they came upon an unusually large building, prompting her to ask, "Why is this building so large?" Fifty-two years later, I still remember the angel's response to her question: This building contains all the answers to prayers that people never prayed.

I know it's a hypothetical scenario, but it reveals a powerful truth. God's desire to answer our prayers is unlimited, but how will they be answered unless we pray?

James 5:17 ties the Old Testament figure of Elijah to the power and efficacy of prayer. James compares Elijah to the rest of us mortals when he maintains that Elijah was a man just like us, meaning fully human in all his ways. Despite his humanity, his fervent prayer on Mt. Carmel connected his hand to God, making his prayer supernatural and, thus, him superhuman.

Live a Prayerful Life

If I were to conclude this chapter with all my illustrations of prayer, I would extend the chapter and book by many more pages. I'm committed to prayer; it is my life's breath. As Paul said in Thessalonians, we are to pray without ceasing. (1 Thessalonians 5:17) In modern vernacular, that means, at all times. If your prayer time is limited to a fixed daily schedule of devotional prayer, I doubt you will experience the "superhumanness" of fervent prayer.

Pray during the night.
Pray over your meals.
Pray in your car.
Pray with others.
Pray by yourself.
Pray with your spouse.
Pray with your family.
Pray in the morning.
Pray when there is an emergency.
Pray when things are going great.

Pray when things are falling apart.

Return to the unbroken communion God desired with us from the beginning. Pray always. A friend of mine told me she hated doing the dishes. One day she decided to turn her hours at the sink into prayers for her friends' families. God's responses to her prayers made dish duty a delight.

Don't be surprised when God's answers aren't the same as your prayers. His ways aren't your ways. (Isaiah 55:8) As mentioned, remember that Jesus' prayer to remove the cup of suffering from Him went unanswered. Nonetheless, He submitted His will to the Father and trusted His answer no matter the cost to self. (Luke 22:42)

While in Colombia a few weeks ago, I prayed for healing for two back-to-back bronchitis attacks. I expected an immediate improvement in my breathing. Instead, God sent me two doctors. One provided medicine that immediately improved my health, and the other prayed for me, releasing a new dimension of anointing.

Ephesians 3:20 says God will answer your prayers commensurate with your requests but greatly multiplied. The word in Greek that means superabundantly is *hyperekperissou* which means "without measure." Your prayer provides the measure, and God's answer is measureless; it's too big to be measured. Whatever you believe and pray for, God's response will be beyond your imagination.

I always encourage people to pray big because we have a big God. Sometimes, we pray financial prayers that can be accommodated by our budget in case God doesn't come through. It doesn't cost any more money to pray big than to pray small, so pray big. Maybe, just maybe, God is more interested in answering your prayer than you are in praying.

Recently I was reading the biography of Lonnie Frisbee in his book, *The Jesus Revolution, Part One*, with Roger Sachs. Lonnie was the catalyst for the massive Jesus Revolution in the 1970s. On one occasion, he knew that someone in the crowd would be healed of warts. He wanted to start his healing ministry with something significant, and this wasn't the word he hoped would jump-start his healing ministry.

He thought it was ludicrous to ask God for something so small, and evidently, the crowd did as well because they laughed and walked out of the building. When most of the group had dissipated, a young lady walked up to Lonnie with a handful of warts falling off the bottom of her foot. God didn't think warts were insignificant. But it was too late to tell the scoffers that God performed a miracle because they had already left the building.

On a mission to India years ago, I made what I thought was a practical illustration of how we ask small, but God is willing to answer big. Using the analogy of dining out, I said we often order hamburgers when God is willing to give us the biggest steak on the menu. Then we blame God for being forced to eat hamburgers when we wanted steak. I can nearly hear God say, "Don't blame me; I didn't order it; you did!"

As soon as I said it, I realized what a massive faux pas I had just committed. My illustration fell flat when I recalled that most Indians are vegetarians. But my conviction remains the same. Our petitions are often barely above what our ingenuity and provision can handle rather than the immense storehouse of God's provision.

Though children of the King, we too oft act as paupers. The God of the universe is not lacking in resources.

Pray About Everything

Yes, I pray for the miraculous, I pray for the nations, and I pray for people to be healed. But I also pray for things that will bless my family life. Don't forget that you are a spiritual being with practical needs. God is a good Father and is concerned with every detail of our lives (Psalm 37:23), so ask. Times of celebration are important to Him, as observed in the many feasts He proclaimed in the Old Testament and the feast that awaits us in heaven. (Revelation 19)

In 1981, Devi and I moved with our two children from Washington State to Amarillo, Texas. Amarillo is in the Texas Panhandle, a six-hour drive from Amarillo to Dallas. I wanted to take my 10-year-old son, Aaron, to a Dallas Cowboys game on Thanksgiving Day. I was ignorant of how difficult it was on those winning days of the Cowboys to purchase tickets at any price. So, into the prayer closet, I went.

My prayer closet was a walk-in closet that I had turned into a prayer room simply by sitting on the floor and closing the door.

I prayed several times in September and again in October that, somehow, I could get tickets to see the Dallas Cowboys play the Chicago Bears on Thanksgiving Day. I hasten to mention that no one knew my prayer. Devi and I pre-determined that since we were new to Texas and didn't have family in the area, we would spend Thanksgiving Day in Dallas, but the Cowboys weren't included in the plans.

In mid-October, my wife, Devi, got a call from a man in our church who owned one of the Christian bookstores in the city. A newly published author was coming to his bookstore to sign books. In preparation for the book signing, the proprietor called to see if my wife would host the event. She gladly volunteered because she, too, wanted to meet the new author.

Devi called me at the office at lunchtime to see if I could take her to lunch. "Of course," I replied, "I would love to." When I arrived at the Book store, I was immediately escorted to the new author busily signing autographs at her book table. When Devi introduced me, the author said, "What do you do?"

"I'm a pastor," I responded.

"Do you know anything about the Book of Job?" she asked, "the Lord told me that the answer to my prayer request is in the Book of Job."

Thankfully I had outlined the entire book of Job and memorized several more pertinent scriptures. After several minutes of sharing insights from Job, the lady asked me if we would soon be in Dallas. "Yes, we will be there on Thanksgiving Day."

"Would you consider being our guests to the Cowboys/Bears game, followed by Thanksgiving dinner afterward?"

I was tempted to say, "Well, we're kind of busy, but we can consider it." Instead, I responded enthusiastically, "We would love to!"

The author's name was Anne Murchison, and her husband, Clint, was the franchise owner of the Dallas Cowboys. On Thanksgiving Day, we accompanied them to Texas Stadium. Nothing is better than being driven to Texas Stadium with the person who built it and owned half the players on the field. We parked in Clint's reserved spot, boarded the elevator to his double-wide suite, and settled in to watch the Cowboys game with the owners.

Talk about an answer to prayer. I prayed to purchase tickets at the box office or buy them from scalpers so we could sit in the nose-bleed section. God's idea was to multiply my prayer and seat us with the owners in his double-wide suite, drinking Coke and eating popcorn, while my son Aaron sat next to Clint Murchison.

After the Cowboys won the game, Anne Murchison took Aaron to the locker room and had the players sign his autograph book. Afterward, we followed them home to enjoy their invitation to a lavish Thanksgiving banquet. Need I say God is good?

God is more willing to give to us than we are to receive. But He does bid us participate in the process by asking and believing.

The Abundant Provision of God

While I believe a mentality of prosperity is better than one of poverty, I don't ever want my pursuit of temporal pleasures to outweigh my desire for eternal treasures. If we are not careful, preaching a prosperity gospel can outweigh our desire to see God's kingdom established on earth. I would rather invest in seeing people saved, delivered, and transformed any day than purchasing a bigger home or car.

Can we have both? Of course, but one far outweighs the other. I am consumed with seeking God's kingdom above my own.

Consequently, most of my prayers are directed toward expanding His kingdom and the people who will inherit it. To me, *"Seek first the kingdom of God and his righteousness, and all these things will be added to you"* (Matthew 6:33) is more than a nice scripture to memorize, it is a life motto. Please note that these things will be added to you only after you seek God's kingdom first.

During his lifetime, George Muller, the great evangelist of the 19th century, was known for his rescue and care of over ten thousand orphans in Bristol, England. Notably, he did not solicit money from outside sources but took his requests directly to God. He is known for his fervent prayer life. Muller said that he had personally logged over 50,000 prayer requests in his journal, 30,000 of which were answered the same day or hour.

Charles Inglis, the well-known evangelist, relates the following remarkable incident from George Muller's life:

When I first came to America thirty-one years ago, I crossed the Atlantic with the captain of a steamer who was one of the most devoted men I ever knew; and when we were off the banks of Newfoundland, he said to me: "Mr. Inglis, the last time I crossed here, five weeks ago, one of the most extraordinary things happened that has completely revolutionized the whole of my Christian life. Up to that time I was one of your ordinary Christians. We had a man of God on board, George Muller, of Bristol. I had been on that bridge for twenty-two hours and never left it. I was startled by someone tapping me on the shoulder. It was George Muller."

"Captain," said he, "I have come to tell you that I must be in Quebec on Saturday afternoon." This was Wednesday.

"It is impossible," I said.

"Very well, if your ship can't take me God will find some other means of locomotion to take me. I have never broken an engagement in fifty-seven years."

"I would willingly help you, but how can I? I am helpless."

"Let us go down to the chart room and pray," he said.

I looked at this man and I thought to myself, "What lunatic asylum could the man have come from? I never heard of such a thing."

"Mr. Muller," I said, "do you know how dense this fog is?"

"No," he replied, "my eye is not on the density of the fog, but on the living God, who controls every circumstance of my life."

He went down on his knees, and he prayed one of the most simple prayers. I thought to myself, "That would suit a children's class, where the children were not more than eight or nine years of age." The burden of his prayer was something like this: "O Lord, if it is consistent with Thy will, please remove this fog in five minutes. You know the engagement You made for me in Quebec for Saturday. I believe it is Your will."

When he had finished, I was going to pray, but he put his hand on my shoulder and told me not to pray.

"First," he said, "you do not believe God will do it; and second, I believe He has done it. And there is no need whatever for you to pray about it."

I looked at him, and George Muller said this: "Captain, I have known my Lord for fifty-seven years and there has never been a single day that I have failed to gain an audience with the King. Get up, Captain and open the door, and you will find the fog is gone." I got up, and the fog was gone. On Saturday afternoon George Muller was in Quebec. *

Though God can, He has chosen to do nothing except in response to prayer. That boggles the mind. When we pray, it brings us into partnership with Him. He allows us to be participants in the miraculous, not just observers.

In 1 Kings 18:42, the prophet Elijah began his prayer vigil to ask for rain. At his command, his servant scanned the heavens for clouds and a sign of rain. Nothing. Nada. Zero. Not a trace.

On the seventh time searching the heavens, the servant reported seeing a cloud as small as a man's hand. That was enough for Elijah; after forty-two months of drought, a cloud the size of a man's hand was his answer to prayer. He commanded his servant to *"Go and tell Ahab, 'hitch up your chariot and go down before the rain stops you'"* (1 Kings 18:44). What rain, where? But no sooner did he proclaim these words of faith than the sky grew black, and the rain began

---

* From An Hour With George Müller: the Man of Faith to Whom God Gave Millions. Edited by A. Sims. Grand Rapids, Mich.: Zondervan Publishing House, ©1939.

to pour. God doesn't need a big cloud to produce a downpour, just a prayer the size of a man's hand.

You've heard people say, "Well, you've tried everything else, so try praying." Prayer should never be a last resort but our first recourse.

James 4:2 makes it painfully clear; we don't have because we don't ask. Let's be the ones who are committed to praying until revival comes. Let's be the ones who echo the request of the first disciples: *"Lord, teach us to pray"* (Luke 11:11).

CHAPTER 8
CONTEND FOR THE MIRACULOUS

"Now many signs and wonders were regularly done among the people by the hands of the apostles" (Acts 5:12).

"Behold, I have given you authority to tread on serpents and scorpions, and over all the power of the enemy, and nothing shall hurt you" (Luke 10:19).

One of the greatest lies the devil ever perpetrated on the church is the doctrine of dispensationalism, which states that signs, wonders, miracles, and gifts of the Spirit were abandoned when the Bible became a closed canon. The argument is that when John wrote his "Amen" in the book of Revelation, the activity of the Holy Spirit became dormant, except for an occasional inclusion in a creed or at the end of a prayer. Otherwise, He was finished once John lifted his pen from the parchment.

Can you imagine having to combat the forces of Satan's domain without the leadership and empowerment of the

Holy Spirit? I think I'll apply for another profession if I'm a minister.

Not only was the Holy Spirit effectively silenced, but His power was limited only to the early church. The rest of the church age has had to do without what propelled the gospel into the world within a few centuries of its inception. What an ingenious ploy of the devil and theologians to suggest those days are over. Not only was the Holy Spirit relegated to being God Junior, but His immense power, demonstrated in the raising of Jesus from the dead, was disposed of as unnecessary and carried on only by fringe elements and fanatics. Of course, Pentecostals and charismatics are at the top of the list of ignorant fanatics. Guilty as charged.

In his book Spirit Hermeneutics, Craig S. Keener (whom I will quote from again further in this chapter) states:

When we approach the Bible simply to prove what we already believe, we are not beginning with the fear of the Lord. Loyalty to Scripture means valuing its teaching above any other doctrinal commitments that may not actually flow from that.

In the past several centuries, biblical scholars have consistently downplayed the necessity of the gifts of the Spirit, including all supernatural activity and their validity. What was common in the early church, even centuries after John finished his vision on the island of Patmos, has been covered over by the bias of clergy who have predetermined that God no longer works in the miraculous, as demonstrated by Jesus and carried on by His disciples.

I firmly believe their resistance and insistence that the gifts of the Spirit and the miraculous are no longer available to the church is because of the lack of it in their ministries. They preach against what they do not experience.

A Matter of Worship

With the proliferation of study Bibles, online Bible courses, and many media preachers and teachers from the past two centuries, this unholy, unbiblical doctrine continues to infect and influence the body of Christ. To echo Keener, doctrinal commitments supersede the fear of the Lord. We would rather stand on the safe ground of what we can explain by reason than open ourselves to a God who is wholly unlike us and operates in the miraculous.

When Jesus addressed the Samaritan woman at the well in John 4:24, He said, *"God is spirit, and those who worship him must worship in spirit and truth."* Read that again. When you try to imagine the vastness of God, do you imagine a giant man on a throne? God looks nothing like you and me. He is spirit. We cannot fathom what He looks like, for nobody can look at Him and live (Exodus 33:20). Therefore, when we worship God, we *must* worship Him in spirit because He is spirit! This is why God sent His Spirit to us, that we may have His fullness dwelling in us and enabling us to operate in every single gift He offers. It is our true act of worship to serve Him and perpetuate His works in this world.

The Bible says that Satan is the father of lies (John 8:44) and, since the beginning, has desired worship. He even demanded that Jesus worship him in exchange for the kingdoms of the world (Matthew 4:9–11). If he can perpetuate the lie that the Spirit of God, with the blessings of all His gifts, is useless to us, the very gift Jesus died to give us (John 16:7), he can keep us from true worship.

THE ACCESS TO POWER

Remember Jesus' reply to the devil, *"Be gone, Satan! For it is written, 'You shall worship the Lord your God and him only shall you serve'"* (Matthew 4:9). As I've said before, Jesus knew that what you worship you will serve. The devil wants nothing more than for people to serve him.

If you need further proof that the devil is stopping up the gifts of God to keep us from worshipping God, look no further than to the Scriptures themselves:

*"But if all prophesy, and an unbeliever or outsider enters, he is convicted by all, he is called to account by all, the secrets of his heart are disclosed, and so, falling on his face, he will **worship God** and declare that God is really among you* (1 Corinthians 14:24–25, emphasis added).

When the invisible gifts of God are visible to men, it leads to the worship of God! No wonder the devil wants to stop the body of Christ from operating in the gifts.

Human Commentary

When something is put into print, it becomes believable. Most people do not take the time to research and refute the argument of dispensationalism and take it de facto. Thus, when a respected teacher adds a note at the bottom of their study Bible that says, "The gifts and miracles of the Holy Spirit have not existed since the closing of the New Testament Canon," we falsely believe, who can argue with that? After all, they assume, it's in the Bible.

Incorrect. It is not in the Bible. It's in the study notes beneath the heavy black line denoting the conclusion of the sacred text and the beginning of human commentary. It's in the biased footnotes of scholars that make unbiblical and outlandish statements.

I tell students of the Bible to watch out for the dark black line at the bottom of the study Bible. Above the black line, God is talking, and under the black line, man is commenting on what God has said. Above the black line, you can be sure of its veracity, but under it, it may or may not be accurate or even partially true. God the Holy Spirit and the Bible do a good job defining and describing what it means, but you cannot always be so sure with man's commentaries.

Commentaries and notes are only sometimes reliable and, in some cases, blatantly at odds with the Scripture. I appreciate and use Bible commentaries and value the study notes included in many current study Bibles. However, it is essential to remember that there is not one commentator who has not, at one time or another, written notes and comments that are contrary to the Bible. Though this is well meaning, once the Scripture hits the scholar's mind, comments, and computer, it is no longer infallible. There is not one book ever written, except the Bible, which does not include errors, including this one. Be cautious. The doctrines of demons (1 Timothy 4:1) that Paul refers to appear somewhere in print.

The Unchangeable God

God is unchanging. *"For I the Lord do not change"* (Malachi 3:6). What He has determined, He will do (Ezekiel 12:25). From the beginning, the Spirit of God hovered above creation (Genesis 1:2). He has always existed in perfect triune harmony with God the Father and God the Son. The moment God spoke the words, the Spirit brought His desires into being. And so, it is today that the Spirit helps us accomplish God's desires on earth. We can all agree that the church is still in existence today. It makes no sense that the Holy Spirit would withhold His gifts from His beloved church in an ever-darkening world. Worse, those who argue that the gifts of the Spirit have ceased seem very selective about what gifts we are still allowed to use and what we aren't. As Keener states,

This cessationist argument also appears a curious tactic when we consider the selective nature of the reasoning. Would someone argue that the unity of Christ's multi-gifted body would pass away with the completion of the canon unless there is explicit evidence to the contrary (cf. Eph 4:11–13)? Or more analogously, would someone argue that once the canon is complete, we no longer need the gift of teaching? Why some gifts and not others?

Try telling missionaries that the gifts of the Spirit or miracles no longer exist. Most believe they do, and the ones who don't generally return home disillusioned because of their lack of measurable fruit. When dealing with cultures where Satan's works, including witches, witchcraft, idols, curses, and demonic activity, are a common experience, it's either believe God works supernaturally or throw in the towel. Flesh and blood can never counteract demonic activity; case in point, when the seven sons of Sceva tried to exorcise demons from people, the demons turned on them and beat them to a pulp (Acts 19:11–20). You need to trade in any study Bible that doesn't include present-day miracles for one that does. Better yet, return to the original word of God where there is no lack of proof that God's Holy Spirit power is at work then, now, and forever (Zechariah 4:6 and Hebrews 13:8).

There have always been charlatans, false prophets, false miracle workers, and false apostles, but that doesn't negate the real. The enemy always wants to counterfeit the real; he loves attention, so don't give him any. Jesus and the early church warned of these charlatans. However, Jesus also said His disciples would do greater works than He did (John 14:12). There is no proof that Jesus only desired to give gifts to the apostles so they would take them to the grave. This would have been considered utter nonsense to the apostles. The proof lies within 2 Timothy 1:6 when Paul exhorts Timothy to fan the gifts of God within him to flame. In this same letter in chapter 4, he tells him that he will soon die (2 Timothy 4:6). He fully expected Timothy to outlive him and use the gifts God had given him. Why would he bother telling Timothy to fan gifts into flame if they had an expiration date that would die out when Paul did? It makes no sense at all.

Since Jesus Christ is the same yesterday, today, and forever, which Hebrews 13:8 makes clear, there is no cessation of the gifts until Jesus comes. After that, you won't need any. You will know as you are known. When the perfect Jesus comes, there is no more need for words of knowledge, prophecy, tongues, interpretation, or healing.

In saying this, I'm alluding to one of the most incorrectly oft-quoted Scriptures, where opponents of tongues and prophecy attempt to negate them. *"For we know in part and we prophesy in part, but when the perfect comes, the partial will pass away"* (1 Corinthians 13:9–10). The problem is, when these critics negate tongues, they also negate knowledge, which doesn't argue well for them. They try to interpret

Scripture without the aid of knowledge, which disappears simultaneously as tongues and prophecy.

The Bible declares Jesus as the only Perfect One. He was born perfect and attained perfection through His suffering (Hebrews 5:8–9). Since Jesus hasn't returned yet, the gifts of the Spirit continue to operate. The perfect has not yet come. In addition, a careful study of Scripture will reveal prophecy, prophets, and gifts of healing continue to be mentioned from the book of Acts and the Epistles to the book of Revelation. I'm certain that the book of Revelation hasn't been fulfilled yet.

Will Jesus Find Faith on Earth?

For centuries, after the closing of the Canon, the early church fathers continued to record hundreds of examples of miracles and the supernatural activity of the Holy Spirit. The miraculous was common until the church became nationalized, beginning with Constantine in the fourth century. Since then, it has become more sporadic, nearly to extinction. In the last several centuries, with the growing popularity of liberal European theologians' works published and quoted in America, we saw another drastic drop in belief in the miraculous.

Of course, why wouldn't it? If I don't believe something exists, I will most likely never see or experience it. Faith seems to be God's prerequisite for revealing Himself. In the delay until Christ's triumphant return on earth, we must continue to contend, to ask, seek, and knock for the things of God. As Jesus Himself said regarding His delay, *"Nevertheless, when the Son of Man comes, will He find faith on earth?"* (Luke 18:8).

One of the more famous shredders of Scripture was our beloved founding father, Thomas Jefferson. He made his own Bible with scissors and glue by removing anything detailing the miraculous. After excising everything miraculous, he had hardly anything left in the Bible, including his faith. As a Deist, miracles are not necessary, especially the revelation of God Himself.

The Charismatic Movement

On April 8, 1966, *Time* magazine ran the infamous, first-ever black cover reading, "Is God Dead?" Evidently not because *Time* issued another striking cover on June 21, 1971, this time glaringly psychedelic, that read, "Jesus Revolution," chronicling the massive Jesus revival that started on the West Coast and eventually covered the nation and abroad.

Not mentioned in the *Time* article was the most significant move of the Spirit in church history that began six years earlier, in 1960, at an Episcopalian church in Van Nuys, California, under the leadership of Father Dennis Bennett. His book *Nine O'Clock in the Morning*, chronicling his baptism with the Holy Spirit, helped spread what became known as the Charismatic Renewal. This became national, as the Jesus Revolution essentially was, and global.

It soon spread to other mainstream Protestant denominations, including Lutherans and Presbyterians, by 1962, and to Roman Catholicism by 1967. Methodists became involved in the charismatic movement in the 1970s. It is estimated that fifty million people in virtually all denominations experienced the presence and power of the

Spirit from 1960 to 1980. I'm sure we will never know the actual number, but it was the biggest move of the Spirit since the day of Pentecost.

Evangelical scholars in America refer to the past movements of the Holy Spirit as "Great Awakenings" while completely glossing over the greatest awakening, the charismatic movement. However, if you were to add the numbers of all the past Great Awakenings, they wouldn't be a fraction of what God did in the two decades between 1960 and 1980.

I will never forget when Devi and I attended a Catholic prayer meeting at Gonzaga University in Spokane, Washington, in the late sixties. The room was filled with hundreds of Catholic nuns and priests, singing, worshiping God, speaking in tongues, and dancing before Him. My first thought was, this can't be happening; they're Catholic, upon which God reminded me He hadn't asked my opinion or permission on whom to pour His Spirit out.

God is never at a loss to know how to bring revival to a dead and dying church, including changing our unbelief to belief and our tradition to spontaneous worship and praise. I can hardly wait to see who God will bring in during the last global harvest of souls. We'll see more activity on the street called "Straight" (referring to Paul's conversion to the faith in Acts 9). I pray that God will sovereignly save, call, and send out leaders whom we consider beyond salvation and even blasphemous. God loves to mess up our religious system and traditions. As Dr. Ted Roberts, a great man of God and friend of mine, quipped, "God loves to turn our sacred cows into hamburger." Rather than criticizing churches that do not believe the gifts of the Spirit are for today, pray for them. Who knows? Maybe a Dennis Bennett is within those walls about to experience God's power.

A God of Miracles

I encountered the supernatural power of God as a ten-year-old boy. My dad built a special screened-in porch attached to our Fresno, California, house to keep me cool as my fever soared during the hot days of the California summer. I had kidney failure, and the doctors could not stabilize me. Kidney transplants were unheard of, and air conditioners were rare. Everything had failed, and I was as skinny as a rail. I had trouble keeping food down. Even water would come up.

One day I told my mother that there was a healing evangelist in town, and I wanted to go and have him pray for me. In addition, I boldly proclaimed that I would be healed when he laid his hands on me.

On a hot summer evening in 1952, they took me to a huge tent where the revival was being held. Because I was too weak to stand up, they took a folding chair for me to sit on. When it came time to pray for the sick, I couldn't go to the evangelist, but he came to me. The moment he laid his hands on me, I was healed. Not one more minute, day, or week of fever and soaring temperatures. Not one more day with kidney issues. And as you can see in recent photos, I have kept food down.

God is a God of miracles. We should expect them. The word *supernatural* doesn't exist in the Bible because, with God, everything is natural. I believe we experience the miraculous many more times than we think. Since we only see things in the earthly realm, we tend to think anything beyond that doesn't exist in real life, and if it does, it is rare.

God's Invisible Realm

The invisibility of God's heavenly realm is intentional; He desires us to choose Him by faith now while He remains hidden from sight. It's the way He loves; He will not force our love. He also knows that when we see His Son face-to-face, we will have no choice but to bow and confess that Jesus is Lord, no matter what we believed on this earth (Philippians 2:10). God's invisible realm is so dynamic and powerful that if we saw it, we would be awestruck.

We must be reminded of Elisha's words to his servant when they found themselves surrounded by the Syrians: *"Those who are with us are more than those who are with them"* (2 Kings 6:16). With that, Elisha prayed. The Lord opened the servant's eyes to see that horses and chariots of fire surrounded them in the invisible realm. It's interesting to me that when Elisha, the prophet who was to have double the miracles of Elijah, saw the supernatural army, he witnessed multiple chariots of fire. Because it was an army, thousands of horses and chariots could have been in the revelation. When Elijah was taken to the heavens, he had only one chariot. Elisha had hundreds or thousands at his disposal.

Further, remind yourself of the Scripture in Hebrews 12:1 that tells us a great cloud of witnesses surrounds us. The saints who have passed on now witness our race until we join them in God's heavenly realm, an encouraging and comforting thought.

There's also incredible atmospheric activity in the

heavens. God's throne is surrounded by lightning, fire, and brilliant light (Ezekiel 1). Incidentally, God's throne also has a rainbow around it (Revelation 4:3). When God looks down on His creation, it is through a rainbow. Perhaps this is why He chose a rainbow to remind us of His promise never to flood the earth again. When we look up and see a rainbow of promise, He looks down through His.

Do Not Lose Heart

I would be remiss if I did not acknowledge that I have had hundreds of prayers where I didn't see immediate answers. I pray, nonetheless. 2 Corinthians says, *"So we do not lose heart. Though our outer self is wasting away, our inner self is being renewed day by day. For this light momentary affliction is preparing for us an eternal weight of glory beyond all comparison, as we look not to the things that are seen but to the things that are unseen"* (2 Corinthians 4:16–18).

While we may not see the desired results, we are reminded to continue to look beyond this present earthly life to the eternal glory we will one day enjoy. Further, unanswered prayers do not negate that the God of heaven is, to this day, revealing Himself in the miraculous, and we need to contend for it. We cannot reach the world without a demonstration of the Word and the Holy Spirit's power. Intellectual knowledge of the Bible isn't enough. It must be confirmed with signs, wonders, and miracles, as Paul reminded the Corinthians: *"And I was with you in weakness and in fear and much trembling, and my speech and my message were not in plausible words of wisdom, but in demonstration of the Spirit and of power so that your faith might not rest in the wisdom of men, but in the power of God"* (1 Corinthians 2:3–4).

Maybe if we prayed earnestly, as the early church did in Acts 4:29–31, our houses of worship would also be filled with the Holy Spirit and shake under the power of God. I would love to see God mess up our tradition.

I am fascinated and inspired by reading the biography of Lonnie Frisbee, the young hippie from Haight Ashbury who was the catalyst for the youth revival in the 1960s and 70s that we call the Jesus Revolution. Though Lonnie wasn't wanted once miracles began to appear, he shook churches, cities, and nations for Jesus. Thousands of people were introduced to Jesus, healed, delivered from demons, and set on fire for God. The three volumes of books on Lonnie's life, *The Jesus Revolution*, by Roger Sachs, chronicle the testimonies of the many people transformed through his preaching. We have not witnessed such a major outpouring of the Holy Spirit for over forty years. I long to see this again in my lifetime.

In the late seventies, I attended a Kathryn Kuhlman meeting in Seattle, Washington. Thousands waited hours to get in, and thousands were turned away. There was such a sense of the pervading presence of the Holy Spirit that it was nearly palpable. People, by the hundreds, were being healed. As I sat there, tears filled my eyes at what God was doing. As I sat quietly, meditating on what was going on, I sensed God say to me, "In the last days, the move of my Spirit will be so great there will no longer be just a few preachers with a healing ministry, but multitudes of people releasing my healing power." I had the distinct feeling that the age of the one-person show was over. It sounds crass to call it a show, but you know what I mean. Sometimes you couldn't tell who was getting the credit, and it should always be God!

From that day until this, the prophecy of Habakkuk continually comes to my spirit: *"The earth will be filled with the knowledge of the glory of the LORD as the waters cover the sea"* (Habakkuk 2:14).

Likewise, the prophecy of Joel 2, repeated by Peter in Acts 2, rings in my heart that God will pour His Spirit on all flesh in the last days. If the last days commenced two thousand years ago, the prophecy is as relevant today as it was then, possibly more so.

I pray that the Lord will let me see it with my own eyes and experience it in my life and ministry. I need a divine earthquake. The church of the twenty-first century needs a shaking. We need revival. I am unwilling to live a powerless life devoid of your miraculous. I will contend for the miraculous. I want the real stuff.

It's time we have a new *Time* magazine cover that reads: "The entire globe is seeing the glory of the Lord." I hope that's okay with those who don't believe it can happen.

CHAPTER 9
CONCENTRATE ON YOUTH

"And it shall come to pass afterward, that I will pour out my Spirit on all flesh; your sons and your daughters shall prophesy, your old men shall dream dreams, and your young men shall see visions" (Joel 2:28).

"The names of the twelve apostles are these: first, Simon who is called Peter, and Andrew his brother; James the son of Zebedee, and John his brother, Philip and Bartholomew; Thomas and Matthew the tax collector; James the son of Alphaeus, and Thaddaeus; Simon the Zealot, and Judas Iscariot, who betrayed him" (Matthew 10:2–4).

As much as I enjoy movies on Christ's life, we have done ourselves an injustice in many ways. Usually, Jesus is portrayed as a Caucasian male surrounded by other Caucasian males—all around the age of thirty. In actuality, Jesus was a Hebraic Jewish man of Middle Eastern descent, and most scholars believe the disciples ranged in age from thirteen (yes, you read that correctly) to thirty.

Gabriel Zamora, the President of Kingdom Global Ministries and a leading authority of youth in the church, believes that as many as ten of the original twelve disciples were teenagers, Peter and Judas being the only exceptions. Gabriel's conclusion is based on the Roman tax. The tax applied to all adult males over eighteen, and all but Peter and Judas weren't taxed. (Matthew 17:24–27, Exodus 30:14–15) Read through this lens, Scriptures such as these begin to make sense:

"And when his disciples James and John saw it, they said, "Lord, do you want us to tell fire to come down from heaven and consume them?" But he turned and rebuked them" (Luke 9:54–55).

"And James and John, the sons of Zebedee, came up to him and said to him, 'Teacher, we want you to do for us whatever we ask of you.' And he said to them, 'What do you want me to do for you?' And they said to him, 'Grant us to sit, one at your right hand and one at your left, in your glory'" (Mark 10:35–37).

Sounds like a bunch of teenagers to me. Some of Jesus' responses make sense too:

"How long shall I stay with you? How long shall I put up with you? Bring the boy here to me" (Matthew 17:17 NIV).

"Little children, yet a little while I am with you" (John 13:33).

If Jesus was unafraid to shape, mentor, love, correct, and live His life surrounded by youth, why are we so afraid? Yes, they'll get it wrong, but didn't you? I can think of a thousand ways I misread a situation in my youth. Youth will want to misuse power (calling down fire, elevating their position); so do adults. They'll challenge, question, and frustrate. So do adults. But much as the disciples, once lovingly shaped, they can become world changers.

In the Jewish culture, children become men and women at thirteen. In the ritual of the Bar Mitzvah, the boy reads aloud, "Today I become a man." What if we viewed youth with the end in mind? What if we began to view them as the vibrant men and women they will become? How would that change the way we elevate and involve them within the church?

A Prophetic Vision

A friend strolled mindlessly through the mall to cool down on a hot day. As she passed yet another storefront with photographs displaying teens dressed in next to nothing, she heard the Lord say, "They're devaluing my youth." If we don't value teens enough to give them a vision other than the one the world offers, what will they become? The evidence is all around; brace yourself for some devastating statistics:

o Ninety-four percent of teens have watched pornography by the age of fourteen, just 6 percent shy of 100 percent.

o Between 2016 and 2020, drug use among eighth graders rose by 61 percent.

o Suicide is the second-leading cause of death among teenagers and young adults.

o The United States has one of the highest teen pregnancy rates in the Western industrialized world.

o This year, seven hundred and fifty thousand girls will give birth, mostly out of wedlock.

o Eight out of ten dads don't wed the mother of their child.

If those statistics didn't affect you deeply, I suggest you reread them. According to George Barna, the guru of modern spiritual and cultural research, Gen-Z is the first post-Christian generation in American culture. According to the Pinetop Foundation's research, "Every year, over one million young people will walk away from the Christian faith."

Statistics on youth involvement in the modern church run the gamut from disappointing to disastrous. In one statistic, half of all youth in the church will not return to church by the fall school semester. That's hundreds of thousands of teens who will simply fall away. The reasons vary:

I went to college.

I'm not interested.

Church doesn't relate.

Church is boring.

I don't believe in God.

I would rather be with my friends.

It's just for older people.

Our generation doesn't need it.

It sounds like we have let the world shape their vision of what a vibrant life is and isn't. Proverbs 29:18 says, "Where there is no prophetic vision the people cast off restraint, but blessed is he who keeps the law." Another version of this reads that the people will perish without a vision. Our youth are perishing. While I don't believe church leaders are responsible for this massive exodus of young people from the church, I do believe that, like leaders in any organization, they must carry the burden and contend for a prophetic vision.

Give Them Purpose

Most churches have tried to keep up with the younger generation by adopting current music, cool lighting, fog machines, programs, and contemporary youth bands. All these things can be good if they aren't the focus. Youth also want substance. They want to be challenged. They want a purpose in life that makes sense of what they are going through. They want to be radical. They want to be heard, not just seen. They want to be discipled. They want something to die for. Most importantly, they want to be loved for who they are.

If you look at many mainline churches today, the aging population takes up most of the pews, consumes most of the program, is the most visibly seen on the platform, and is most influential in determining the course, conviction, and community of the church. Rarely are youth consulted to ask what their opinion is. Consequently, in the minds of the youth, the church is essentially uninterested in them.

As soon as Jesus chose the Twelve, He offered them a vision; He immediately called them apostles. Wow! Who would condone that today? They hadn't been to seminary or had twenty years of ministry experience. Furthermore, they hadn't endured a twenty-four-week leadership training curriculum, which, by our way of thinking, would immediately disqualify them. And, of course, we would check their giving record to ensure they tithed.

I love Mark Twain's tongue-in-cheek quote about youth: "Too bad that youth is wasted on the young."

Debilitating Attitudes:

There's a debilitating attitude amongst many older people toward the youth:

They can't be trusted with responsibility.

They should be seen but not heard.

They will have to wait until they are more mature before they're allowed to participate in the church.

Don't be bothered with them.

Wait until they grow up. After all, it's risky using youth.

Their brash youthfulness might drive people away from the church.

We can't afford to lose any more tithers.

What if they aren't professional enough? How will the church or leadership perceive them?

More importantly, if they fail, will that cast a shadow on our leadership?

Unless we include the youth in the church today, there will be no youth in the church tomorrow. It's more serious than that. Unless we include the youth in the church today, there will be no church tomorrow. Once the older generation has died out, there is no church.

Since retiring from pastoral ministry in 2002, I have been involved in full-time global mission work. That means I have been in hundreds of churches from all denominational and nondenominational backgrounds. In most churches, the congregation's aging population fills the pews. Youth attendance is minimal or absent. I look around, and there is hardly anyone who doesn't have gray hair. Where is the youth?

When did you last see a young person preach the Word in church? I can hear someone say, "They must be tested first." Well, then, when are you going to let them be tested? If not now, when?

When has the leadership consulted any youth to hear their opinion or how they can be released into the ministry? They don't need to preach a sermon. Why not just let them share their testimony? Or participate in the worship band? Or pray? Or make the announcements? Or greet people at the door?

To get more personal, when did you last have young people around your kitchen table? And if they were present, were they silent listeners or active participants?

We should release youth into ministry rather than safely continue to use the tried-and-true professional clergy or older folks. Who cares if the youth fail? All the disciples of Jesus failed, but He delegated His authority to them anyway.

Without giving youth a significant voice in your church, your church will always lack a certain attractive draw, magnetism, and enthusiasm. We let them go on short-term mission trips where they can preach to the heathen and pat ourselves on the back when we allow them to give a ten-minute report. But to preach in their church is rarely heard of.

Involve Children in Church

Last year I was in Pastor Alvaro Retes' church in Chile. A child opened the service in prayer and concluded the service. The worship band was made up of youth. The pastor's own family was integrally involved in all aspects of the church's life. It was powerful. It was genuine. It was inviting. It was electric. It was full of the Holy Spirit. Most importantly, it was full of youth.

Last year, I was also in a Brazilian church in Boca Raton, Florida, where Ana Paula and Gustavo Bessa are pastors. Youth filled the front of the church, the aisles, the platform, and the pews. Talk about excitement. Youth were continually being saved and filled with the Holy Spirit. Teens wrote their own praise and worship music and led worship. Creativity was everywhere. The Holy Spirit heavily graced the church atmosphere, and I basked in it.

I spoke at a men's conference of several thousand in Salvador, Brazil. The pastor, Milton Ebenezer de Souza, regularly releases all his children to minister in the church and has been doing so for years. He also exposes the congregation to the wisdom of his eighty-four-year-old father from time to time. Years ago, as he laid hands on people during the altar ministry, he noticed his ten-year-old daughter walking along with him, doing the same. It's no wonder his children serve in the church rather than give their talents to the world.

In writing this chapter, I reflected on my childhood. I was genuinely born again at four years old. I was baptized in water and the Holy Spirit when I was five. I remember those years vividly. My parents had moved from a small rural town to a much larger city, and the church they attended had a special series of services where the evangelist preached on the baptism in the Holy Spirit. I remember going to the front when he gave the invitation, laying hands on people, and praying for them to receive the fullness of the Holy Spirit. Five years old. And, amazingly, they were filled. That was before children were shuttled off to separate rooms where they could learn at their age level. My parents felt I could learn much by being with them, worshiping with them, and listening to the preacher. They didn't allow me to play games during the service; I had to pay attention to what was being said, so I was also taught how to behave in the house of God. As soon as I learned to write, I began to take notes of the sermon. My, how times have changed.

Due to this, I had a ravenous desire to learn the Word of God. I began memorizing Scripture and walking to school with Scripture cards to learn more about the Word.

I understand the need for Bible classes designed to teach younger children. There have also been some adverse effects, including children never being able to worship with their parents, hear the corporate Word as it is delivered to the Body, or be exposed to the larger body of Christ. I noticed a sign in the First Baptist Church in Dallas, Texas, where a section was roped off, designated for parents with children who wanted to worship with them. What a great idea.

Light Your Candles

Three parables in Luke 15 describe something lost. In the first parable, it is a lost sheep. In the third and most well-known parable, it's a lost son. But the second and lesser-discussed parable depicts a woman who loses one of her ten coins. Jesus describes her lighting a candle and diligently searching for it.

What is curious about the parable is where the coin was lost, in the house. Is it possible that in today's church, we have a lot of lost coins, children and youth who grow up in the church but have no actual encounter with the living Lord? They spend their lives, from the cradle to their teens, being shuttled from class to class but don't know God or His Son. Is it possible we have raised a generation of children and youth who attend Sunday school weekly but don't know Jesus? I fear we may have some lost "children coins" in the house.

In today's church culture, we have sent our youth to side rooms, back rooms, off-campus rooms, game rooms, entertainment rooms, and even some drab, uninviting rooms. They can easily feel alienated and possibly abandoned by the generations ahead of them. Unless they are part of the adult church, they will never feel comfortable in church. The same is true for different races. If diversity is not represented on the platform, diversity will not be seen in the pews. And it cannot be mere tokenism that people can spot a mile away. It must be an authentic, pure love. Our love can have no ulterior motives, such as church growth, increased income, or political correctness.

In many of our churches, youth are shuttled off to educational programs and are unseen again until they graduate high school. Some churches even extend the seclusion into early adulthood. Every child has their own church, but they have never known what it is like to worship or hear the Word in an adult environment. They don't have the joy of worshipping with their parents. They have no interaction with the leaders of the church. They have never heard the pastor preach. They spend their entire lives in children's church, even up and through the teen years and sometimes beyond. Is it any wonder they have no interest in attending the adult church, and when they are out of high school, they disappear into the world? We are producing generations of spiritually illiterate children raised in the church who do not know God or His power. We have lost coins in the house, and no one is desperately searching for them. Someone needs to light a candle.

Deuteronomy 6:6–9 gives steps to childhood biblical education:

"And these words that I command you today shall be on your heart. You shall teach them diligently to your children, and shall talk of them when you sit in your house, when you walk by the way and you lie down, and when you rise. You shall bind them as a sign on your hand, and they shall be as frontlets between your eyes. You shall write them on the doorposts of your house and on your gates."

In other words, every aspect of our lives should model the Word of God. Young people led one of the greatest revivals in America's history, and I firmly believe they will again.

The Youth Want Older People

Are you willing to get your feathers ruffled and do things differently? Friends of mine approaching sixty began attending a church in their city focused on youth. He and his wife embraced the loud music and flashing lights because they could sense a hunger and thirst for the Word of God among the young people they hadn't witnessed in many years. This couple didn't think the youth would want much to do with them because of their age, but soon kids were approaching *them*:

"Hey, can I hit you up for coffee?"

"When I preach, I look at you to see if you're nodding, then I know I'm on the right track."

"Can you help me? I slept with my boyfriend, and I'm scared."

Before they knew it, their lives were full of hangouts with pierced and tattooed teens, and they loved every minute. When the leadership in the church had a crisis, my friends were on hand to counsel them through it. Youth need spiritual moms and dads. Will you be there for them with open arms?

In the last days, God will pour out His Spirit on the youth. If we want revival, we must begin opening our doors to the youth. It is promised in Joel 2 and repeated in Acts 2 as a sign of the last days. Surely, these days have arrived.

As I conclude this important chapter, I have invited Gabriel Zamora, my successor as the President of Kingdom Global Ministries and a leading youth evangelist and consultant in the nation, to add his perspective. These are the words of Gabriel:

In 2020–2021 America experienced what felt like a renaissance of racism and division at a heart-wrenching level. I am not white. I am not Black. In many ways, I am part of the overlooked minority. I am Latino. I have not experienced the extreme of what my Black brothers and sisters in America have, but I can empathize with many of the injustices of everyday treatment because of how I look.

Years ago, I walked into an Apple Store from the construction site. My boots were covered in mud, and my face was sun scorched. I didn't smell like roses. Every worker completely ignored me. The security guard following me around the store was the only one who gave me attention. This may not be a big deal to those who have never experienced this, but when it's your hundredth time being treated like an outsider that doesn't belong, it's infuriating.

I have been held at gunpoint by the police because a woman called the cops and said, "Some Mexican thugs broke into the daycare behind my house." At the time, my mother worked in the daycare and we were helping her change out the toys.

I'm thankful for how far we have come in America concerning racism and fair treatment of all. We have made great strides in becoming more politically correct in our speech. So much so that we must choose our words with the utmost care lest we be canceled by society. We also know we have a long way to go in our language regarding the youth. Hear me; if we were to talk about another ethnicity or people group the way that we talk about the next generation, we would be labeled bigots.

Have you heard some of the things said about young people?
"They're all lazy."
"They're all entitled."
"This generation is doomed."
"They don't desire the things of God."
"They are so sensitive and weak."
"They are all controlled by their emotions."

"They will never be able to carry the weight of ministry like my generation."

"They are all too liberal and have forsaken holiness."

We have all heard disgruntled leaders say these things. Please hear me; if we speak about people beginning with the words, "They all..." we have already alienated a whole people group that is precious in God's sight. The greater tragedy is that we are denied the pleasure of witnessing the extensive gifts a whole people group has to give to the world.

Let me ask you a question. Do you believe there are young people you know that have something they could contribute to you personally right now? Do you believe there is something you could learn from them? Do they have any traits or insights that could benefit your ministry, and are you open to learning from them? Even in their lack of maturity, could you benefit from their youthful wisdom? If we allowed youth into our world, we could both benefit, making the ministry of both of us more prosperous.

Missionaries do whatever is necessary to speak the people's language; they spend years of study understanding a people group, their ways, and their culture. What if we were to do this with our kids? Immersing ourselves in today's youth and truly understanding their "language"? In the words of a youthful euphemism, maybe you can become a cross-cultural Jedi Master to the next generation. As Psalm 145 says, "Let each generation tell its children of your mighty acts; let them proclaim your power. I will meditate on your majestic, glorious splendor and your wonderful miracles. Your awe-inspiring deeds will be on every tongue; I will proclaim your greatness. Everyone will share the story of your wonderful goodness; they will sing with joy" *(Psalm 145:4–7 NLT).*

INITIATE

God's model for every generation falls beneath two broad categories; to initiate and release.

*The whole goal of discipleship is that all would be blessed through one person. When God wanted to reveal Himself to the world, He **initiated** a relationship with one man, Abraham. This principle runs through the entire Word of God, a person called to be a living example to a people group by passing down the things of God so that all are blessed.*

As I see it, this Scripture is a spiritual model. It's the way God does things. Every generation—the ones before us, after us, and the generation you are a part of right now, has something to proclaim, meditate on, do, and share. Legacy must be communicated. You can't just hope it, think about it, or dream it. God says, "Let each generation tell its children." There must be a passing down. Succession is built into Scripture—a spiritual ancestry of sorts. Legacy moves from generation to generation, from one person to another, from a group of people to another group, and from nation to nation. It's also a narrative or theme that echoes throughout the Bible.

God made a blood covenant with Abraham that would endure from generation to generation, as promised in Genesis 12:2. "I will make you into a great nation. I will bless you and make you famous, and you will be a blessing to others" *(New Living Translation).*

God used Moses to deliver the Jews from 400 years of bondage, free them from slavery, and redeem them. God wanted His people never to forget what happened. He wanted them to remember their legacy.

In Deuteronomy 6:1–3, Moses writes,

These are the commands, decrees, and regulations that
the LORD your God commanded me to teach you. You
must obey them in the land you are about to enter and
occupy, and you and your children and grandchildren must
fear the LORD your God as long as you live. If you obey all
his decrees and commands, you will enjoy a long life. Listen
closely, Israel, and be careful to obey. Then all will go well
with you, and you will have many children in the land
flowing with milk and honey, just as the LORD, the God of
your ancestors, promised you *(New Living Translation)*.

*The theme of God-initiated legacy continues from the Old
Testament to the New Testament. God used Paul to share His plan
with Titus. Paul had much to say about mentorship, discipleship,
and the succession model:*

As for you, Titus, promote the kind of living that reflects
wholesome teaching. Teach the older men to exercise self-
control, to be worthy of respect, and to live wisely…
Similarly, teach the older women to live in a way that
honors God. …These older women must train the younger
women to love their husbands and their children, to live
wisely and be pure, to work in their homes, to do good, and
to be submissive to their husbands. Then they will not bring
shame on the word of God. In the same way, encourage the
young men to live wisely. And you yourself must be an
example to them by doing good works of every kind. Let
everything you do reflect the integrity and seriousness of
your teaching. Teach the truth so that your teaching can't be
criticized *(Titus 2:1–8 New Living Translation)*.

*While exhorting Titus to teach older men and women, he also
tells him to focus on the youth. When we operate with legacy in*

mind, we will always be aware of the connection between the generations.

Legacy Is in God's Heart and Mind

Legacy is what we leave, from our lives and ministries, for future generations. However, that legacy can be bad or good, depending on our works. That is why Paul encouraged believers to build with precious stones and metals rather than wood, hay, or stubble (1 Corinthians 3:12). The purpose of this chapter is to encourage leaders to invest in youth and make them the center of their legacy. We must pass on a legacy of integrity, fruitfulness in Christ, generosity, faithfulness, and godly morality. To affect future generations, we have to invest in them now.

Legacy has always been in the heart and mind of God. The church, especially in America, hasn't done a good job of passing the spiritual baton. How do I know? Because research shows that depression, anxiety, and suicide are at an all-time high. Relational and racial tensions are dividing us around the globe.

We can't wait another moment to ask why all the young people are leaving. What are we telling them about God and His Word causing this disconnect?

We can't sit back and watch as the world changes dramatically. Three million people, mostly young, are moving to urban centers in places around the globe. I believe this is a spiritual setup. God is up to something extraordinary. Historically, every time the younger generation has been attacked, discarded, or on the move, a deliverer arises.

God doesn't care about age, just availability. God used Daniel, a young man, to be bold and faithful in the most secular city of his day. God chose Mary, a virgin who trusted God and agreed to give birth to Jesus. God took a young Jeremiah and made him a prophet to the nations. When Jesus was age twelve, God sent Him to the synagogue to astound the scribes and Pharisees with His wisdom.

God is still appointing and anointing young people today because their response to Him is, "God, use me and let me do something incredible for Your kingdom." God has not had His last word. He wants to use young people.

A Deeper Level of Trust

Let me take you deeper into this concept of legacy. I've shown it to you in Psalm 145, Deuteronomy 6 and 11, and Titus 2. Now I want to reveal it to you in the life of Jesus.

Legacy requires at least two things, and Jesus lived them out daily. Jesus is not just the message we preach but the model we follow. First, He initiated His followers into an intimate relationship. Jesus always did that. Second, He took the disciples to a deeper level of trust. We see this in His relationship with the disciples, the people He encountered, and ultimately with us as believers.

Peter, a disciple of Jesus, was a model as well. He often wrote in his letters to the church, "I come to you by way of reminder" (2 Peter 1:13). He didn't want them to forget what Jesus said, commanded them to do, and what the early church did daily. Their mission was to tell the story and share their legacy from generation to generation.

This Generation Awaits a Legacy

Just as Peter did, I want to remind you—a spiritual Post-it note of sorts. Legacy is God's idea and His plan. When things aren't going well, we need to change something. We need a course correction. There's no question about that. We need to get back to the biblical model of legacy through relationships. Remember

Psalm 145: "Let each generation tell its children." *Telling is communicating. Communicating involves relationships. A relationship begins when one person initiates or begins the process. That's the case with legacy.*

The Principle of Initiation

The biblical principle in Malachi 4 is that God turns the hearts of the fathers to the sons. One person must initiate the relationship. Thus, the father disciples the son; the mentor chooses the disciple, not vice versa.

Elijah started the relationship with Elisha. Jesus chose His disciples for greater intimacy. Paul took the step with Timothy to include him in his travels. He also later became the friend of Onesimus, a prisoner, and wrote a letter for him to Philemon.

The church has not followed this kingdom principle. Instead, they have adopted a corporate ideology that says you must jump through hoops to get to a person to talk to you. You've got to go through the receptionist, who asks the assistants, who looks at the calendar and lets you know, six months later, what's required to have a few moments with the person you want to meet.

I remember being a teenager full of passion and zeal to live for the Lord. I knew I needed a spiritual father to make it out of my home situation. I needed a mentor. I asked three men in my home church to mentor me. The first one said no because he had his own sons. The second one said no because he didn't have time. The third blew me off and never gave me the dignity of an answer.

What we've created in the church is a generation running after men and women of God, hoping that somehow, some way, they will eventually agree to mentor them. Many are struggling to get a moment, catch a coffee, and hunt the right person down to open the door for them. Let me tell you, that's not mentorship nor how things should work in the kingdom of God. As leaders, who gets access to your life?

Are you following Jesus' example? He invited the disciples into the supernatural power of the transfiguration and the vulnerability of Gethsemane. They got a front-row seat to all the parts of His life. He was the Living Word before them.

We are living letters as believers, men and women of God, and ministry leaders (2 Corinthians 3:2). This generation may not be reading their Bibles, but they are, without a doubt, reading you. So, ask yourself right now, are you initiating? Pause your reading and send a text or a DM (direct message on Instagram, Snapchat, or Facebook). Don't hide behind your assistants or your staff. This message isn't for one of your leaders but for you. Initiate and pour your life out.

Relationship requires proximity. I'm not saying you can't make an impact from a distance; you can. A portion of every mentorship requires face time and quality time. I would venture to say they need to see you correct your kids and make amends with your spouse after minor bickering. They need to see you work hard and play hard. They need to see your scars and celebrate your victories. Legacy doesn't come from veneers or facades. It happens in the bad times and good. In moments of power and vulnerability.

Several months ago, one of my spiritual daughters was with me. Something happened, I got offended, and I was angry. I was ready to hit the person. I didn't do it, however. We got in the car, and she saw how livid I was. Then something changed. I leaned into God's grace and responded in peace. Legacy is passed on as we live out our lives with others.

It says in 2 Timothy 1:6, "This is why I remind you to fan into flames the spiritual gift God gave you when I laid my hands on you" *(New Living Translation). You must be close to lay hands on someone. Paul writing to Timothy reminds him again, in 2 Timothy 3:10:* "But you, Timothy, certainly know what I teach, and how I live, and what my purpose in life is. You know my faith, my patience, my love, and my endurance" *(New Living Translation).*

I don't think I am alone in feeling that initiating a relationship can sometimes be intimidating. It's not easy to be vulnerable with other leaders, young people, and those we choose to mentor. People don't need a cardboard figure or plastic image. They need you. They need your gift. They sure don't need another podcast to listen to. They need a pastor. They need a mentor. How do I know?

For the three men that rejected me, God gave me three others that were unequivocally a part of intimately forming me. The first was Martine Gurule, the youth leader in my home church; the other two men were Larry Titus and Larry Acosta. Their names are here because I must give honor where honor is due.

Larry Titus was everything I needed, and he was there for me. I wanted a voice that cut through the static. He was that man for me. He spoke the truth without offense. He extended unadulterated grace and compassion. He did it with humility. He passed on a legacy to me throughout his life that he's still doing today.

1 *Corinthians 4:15–16 says,* "For even if you had ten thousand others to teach you about Christ, you have only one spiritual father. For I became your father in Christ Jesus when I preached the Good News to you. So, I urge you to imitate me" *(New Living Translation).*

RELEASE

Next, I want you to commit to release. Go back for a moment to Psalm 145 and look at verse 7. "Everyone will share the story of your wonderful goodness; they will sing with joy" *(New Living Translation).*

Sometimes my wife stresses me out. She is seven months pregnant and trying to domesticate our two- and three-year-olds on adult tasks. She wakes up, gets things set up, and lets them cut up food. My son cracks the eggs into the bowl, filling it with both yolks and eggshells. She doesn't care if they make a mess. I do.

"Baby, why don't they have the sippy cup?" I ask.

Calmly she replies, "Because he needs to learn how to drink from a big boy cup." I think, "Why, he's three, and I don't want to clean up all the spills." But she is determined.

"I want them to learn how to do it. They only learn by making messes and figuring it out." That's when I take another deep breath, pray, and release.

We must be releasers in God's kingdom, and share in His plan. 1 Corinthians 1:25–27 says,

This foolish plan of God is wiser than the wisest of human plans, and God's weakness is stronger than the greatest of human strength. Remember, dear brothers and sisters, that few of you were wise in the world's eyes or powerful or wealthy when God called you. Instead, God chose things the world considers foolish to shame those who think they are wise. And he chose things that are powerless to shame those who are powerful. God chose things despised by the world, things counted as nothing at all, and used them to bring to nothing what the world considers important *(New Living Translation)*.

Give This Generation Opportunity

How many of you were someone special when God called you? Not many! We're addicted to this thought of people being "called" and "ready" to serve in the kingdom of God. We think, "They need to go through our discipleship program, then the leadership team, so they can be vetted." Jesus didn't do it that way. He released Peter into ministry before he had it all together, including the revelation that Jesus was the Christ, the Anointed One, and Son of the Living God. He released them before they were ready. Jesus' ministry wasn't just preaching and teaching; He created a relational community. He empowered those around Him. He gave them His authority, letting them go out and use it.

Here's what I know about this generation. They don't lack commitment or purpose. They lack opportunity. They are waiting to be empowered and released. They are waiting for us to say, "Tag! You're it. Go run your race." They will change the world with the message, gifting, and creativity that is unique to them. It may not be the way you'd do it. It's not your methodology, but it's good theology.

Remember, one million youth are leaving the church, not because of disagreement, intellectual barriers, discouragement, or because they can't recognize Jesus in the message. They are leaving the church behind because they are disengaged and haven't been empowered and released into their part in what God is doing. Remember what 1 Timothy 4:11–12 says: "Teach these things and insist that everyone learn them. Don't let anyone think less of you because you are young. Be an example to all believers in what you say, in the way you live, in your love, your faith, and your purity" *(New Living Translation).*

They need an opportunity. If you release them, will they do it as well as you? No. Release them anyway. Are some of them going to take advantage of your influence, authority and get prideful? Absolutely. Release them anyway. They can't mess up what God can't fix. When we refuse to release them, we've made ourselves bigger than God's message and mission.

You have a God-birthed burden for this generation. That conviction leads to responsibility. We are part of the change. Legacy requires of us that we initiate, release, and take responsibility. We are tasked at this critical moment to leave a legacy and shape the church for the future. When Elijah looked at the generation of his day, he wanted to quit. He was discouraged and depressed. He thought he was the only one serving God. The response he got from God was, "There are seven thousand who haven't bowed their knee to Baal" *(1 Kings 19:18). It's not all about you.*

I think God is saying, "Listen. Be encouraged. There's always a remnant. There's still a legacy to be passed on." *He leaves the next steps to us. Will we initiate? Will we release? We will be responsible for whether we did or didn't one day. We are not done. This generation is not finished.*

We will make a difference in the lives of young people. Jesus is the way. He is not the most popular way; He's not the most politically correct way. He's not the Democratic way. He's not the Republican way. He's the way, the truth, and the life. And that message still changes lives. Romans 1:16 declares, "For I am unashamed of this gospel. For it is the power of God unto salvation."

Will You Obey?

Even Saul, the King of Israel, knew what God required. But he refused to do it. Another, David, would. Look at what is written in 1 Samuel 13:13. "'How foolish!' Samuel exclaimed. 'You have not kept the command the LORD your God gave you. Had you kept it, the LORD would have established your kingdom over Israel forever'" (New Living Translation).

God would have established Saul and his kingdom forever, except for one thing. He was disobedient.

In his day, Saul stood head and shoulders above every man. He was good looking and a front-runner for King, chosen by the people of Israel. Samuel anointed him, but Saul was insecure. Often, we think we don't have the gifting, anointing, or belief that God has set us in the position we are in. Let me tell you, legacy needs to come through you. A family and community wait to be renewed because you accepted God's call. There's a city that's being changed forever because you were willing to be used by God. The world needs a legacy. This generation is waiting. Start today.

Thank you, Gabriel, for your insights. You are a treasure trove of valuable insight. Jesus was clear that we cannot enter the kingdom of God unless we become like a child. He often repeated this same theme. If we want to see revival, it is not a matter of children becoming like adults but adults becoming like children.

A few weeks ago, Gabriel launched an interest meeting in anticipation of planting a Kingdom Global Ministries mother church called Home City Church in the Dallas/Fort

Worth, Texas, area. True to his conviction, when it was time to serve communion, he had children distribute the elements and then return to pick up the empty containers. He had youth lead the worship. From the get-go, Gabriel made youth part of this new church plant. The legacy has begun.

CHAPTER 10
PREACH JESUS

"And I, when I am lifted up from the earth, will draw all people to myself" (John 12:32).

"But we preach Christ crucified, a stumbling block to Jews and folly to Gentiles" (1 Corinthians 1:23).

Imagine the scene—disciples of Jesus, most likely bloodied from recent beatings, filthy from dank prison cells, covered in bruises and scuffs—dragged into courts to explain to the Sanhedrin how they healed people and why they continued to preach about a man the rulers had sentenced to death.

Though the disciples' answers varied in content, more often than not, they involved two central themes—first, Christ, His crucifixion, and resurrection. Second, Christ as the promised messiah is found throughout the pages of the Old Testament. When they preached Jesus, they preached Him as the fulfillment of every promise ever given to them.

In William Barclay's book The Making of the Bible, he states:

For long the Church was content with the Old Testament; the Old Testament had become a Christian book. Had not everything that the Old Testament hoped for and foretold come true in Jesus? Had not the great promised Messianic age dawned in him? This was made all the easier because the first Christians were Jews and were, therefore, trained in the technique of the interpretation of Scripture for special purposes.

When the early Jewish believers gathered in homes and dedicated themselves to reading the Word, they were *not* reading the New Testament. They were scouring the pages of the *Old* Testament, using their training to discover Jesus woven throughout their history.

When Jesus walked among the disciples on the road to Emmaus, He explained His sufferings as foretold in the Torah: *"And beginning with Moses and all the Prophets, he interpreted to them in all the Scriptures the things concerning himself"* (Luke 24:27).

When Peter and John stood before the council, they quoted from Psalm 118:22:

Let it be known to all of you and to all the people of Israel that by the name of Jesus Christ of Nazareth, whom you crucified, whom God raised from the dead—by him this man is standing before you well. This Jesus is the stone that was rejected by you the builders, which has become the cornerstone. And there is salvation in no one else, for there is no other name under heaven given among men by which we must be saved (Acts 4:10–12).

Can you imagine the delight of the early disciples every time they discovered Jesus in the pages of the Old

Testament? Even when threatened by the religious people of their day, the disciples wouldn't stop talking about Jesus. So, they were threatened again. But Peter and John answered, *"Whether it is right in the sight of God to listen to you rather than to God, you must judge, for we cannot but speak of what we have seen and heard"* (Acts 4:19–20).

Who Will Preach Christ?

While we preach (and rightly so) from both the Old and New Testament today, we have two crippling tendencies. First, we generally disregard the centrality of Jesus in the Old Testament, robbing modern-day listeners of the same discoveries of the early church. And second, during the past several decades, the church has substituted the preaching of Jesus, His cross, resurrection, and redemption with a feel-good gospel, something that won't offend. It's called being seeker friendly. I call it watering down the gospel. It costs or demands nothing, including repentance. In making Jesus and the cross take a back seat to the current goal of embracing people of all beliefs, the stumbling block of the cross has been battered away in exchange for the vain traditions of man. Repentance and faith in Christ are no longer required.

Several years ago, I recalled hearing Bill Hybels, one of the pioneers in the seeker-sensitive church, openly admit that many people in his congregation were not even born again. It reminded me of Jesus' words to the church at Laodicea: *"For you say, I am rich, I have prospered, and I need nothing, not realizing that you are wretched, pitiable, poor, blind and naked"* (Revelation 3:17). That could be said of many in the American church.

Paul was unwilling to give his life for a powerless gospel devoid of the cross. Neither am I. *"And I, when I came to you, brothers, did not come proclaiming to you the testimony of God with lofty speech or wisdom. For I decided to know nothing among you except Jesus Christ and him crucified"* (1 Corinthians 2:1–2).

Many churches have the latest fog machines, lighting, stage designs, professional singers and musicians, eloquent, charismatic speakers, and, most importantly, coffee shops with real Starbucks coffee. But they lack the presence and power of the Holy Spirit. Rather than lift the name of Jesus, pastors promote a social gospel, a feel-good, neutral, friendly message, and politically correct aphorisms. The Holy Spirit who witnesses Jesus cannot represent or present Him. Programs are highly professional but devoid of the Holy Spirit and His power.

How can we reach the world with the good news of Jesus Christ? We must start by giving precedence to the theme of the *entire* Bible, which is Christology, Christ-centered preaching, and proclamation. Jesus promised that if we exalt Him and His cross, He will draw the world to Himself (John 12:32).

The Preincarnate Christ

For the past several years, I have done extensive study on the preincarnate Jesus, that is, the Jesus of the Old Testament before His incarnation in the New Testament. Throughout the Old Testament, He is revealed in many ways and with different names:

- Angel of the LORD
- YHWH
- The LORD of Hosts
- The Lord (Adon)
- God Elohim
- Eloah
- El
- The God of Israel
- The Husband of Israel
- The Word of the Lord

Preincarnate Jesus is found in virtually every book of the Old Testament. Yet our pulpits rarely teach about Him in any other context except the New Testament. To most readers of the Bible, their only revelation of Jesus is that He is found in the Gospels and the twenty-nine New Testament books. However, YHWH, spelled LORD in most English translations, is mentioned over six thousand eight hundred times in the Old Testament, and many, if not most times, represent Jesus preincarnate, the visible YHWH, God of Israel. (YHWH is pronounced *Yahweh* and is the name God gives Himself in the Old Testament).

When God appears to someone in the Old Testament, it is preincarnate Jesus. We know this because God the Father has never been seen and can never be seen by mortal man. Let me quote a few Scriptures. 1 Timothy 1:17: *"To the King of the ages, immortal, invisible, the only God, be honor and glory forever and ever. Amen."* And 1 Timothy 6:15–16: *"The blessed and only Sovereign, the King of kings and Lord of lords, who alone has immortality, who dwells in unapproachable light, whom no one has ever seen or can see. To him be honor and eternal dominion. Amen."*

Therefore, if God is invisible, it is Christ and not the invisible Most High God and Father of Jesus appearing in the Old Testament encounters. To clinch this truth, read Exodus 33:20; Colossians 1:15; John 1:18; 6:46; 1 John 4:12.

Though God the Father, the invisible YHWH, is mentioned thousands of times in the Old Testament, the visible YHWH, preincarnate Jesus, is likewise mentioned thousands of times and can be easily identified. The I AM of the New Testament is the I AM of the Old Testament. He is the YHWH God that is visible.

Jesus in Genesis

One of my most oft-repeated statements is that the last Adam, Jesus, created the first Adam. Most believers have never heard that Jesus created Adam. He created Adam and Eve and walked and talked with them in the garden. Based on the visibility just discussed, this fact alone defines which member of the Godhead created the first humans. Though all creation originates with God the Father as the Master Architect, God, in His infinite wisdom, chose Jesus to be the Master Builder. *"For by him* [Christ] *all things were created, in heaven and on earth, visible and invisible, whether thrones, dominions, rulers, or authorities—all things were created through him and for him"* (Colossians 1:16). John 1:3 states, *"All things were made through him, and without him was not anything made that was made."*

There is one man I completely envy, Enoch, the seventh from Adam. He walked with God. Can you imagine God, the visible YHWH, preincarnate Jesus, walking with Enoch?

Genesis 5:24 implies they did more than stroll but had sweet communion until the day YHWH took him home. Wow! Lord, can you put me on your visitation list if you still do things like this? *"Enoch walked with God, and he was not, for God took him"* (Genesis 5:24). That is my prayer as well. I want to walk with Jesus in intimacy, then change locations from my house to His someday.

As you study the book of Genesis, you will discover that God appeared to Abraham, Isaac, and Jacob on multiple occasions. Regarding Abraham, YHWH God appeared to him in Ur of the Chaldees, his original home, before Canaan. That is why Abraham wasn't surprised when God visited him in Genesis 18; he had seen Him before on at least two prior occasions. *"Brothers and fathers, hear me,"* Stephen proclaimed on the day of his martyrdom, *"The God of glory appeared to our father Abraham when he was in Mesopotamia, before he lived in Haran"* (Acts 7:2).

God appeared to him in Genesis chapters 12, 15, 17, and 18. And showing His grace, He appeared to Hagar as the "Angel of the Lord," a theophanic (meaning a visible manifestation of God) title for preincarnate Jesus.

Jesus in Exodus

God appeared to Moses multiple times. It doesn't take a scholar to realize that when the God of Israel appeared to Moses in the burning bush in Exodus 3, it had to be Jesus because the invisible YHWH, Father God, has chosen not to be seen by mortal man. Stephen corroborates this in Acts 7:30.

In Exodus 24:9–11, God appeared to Moses and the seventy elders. They "saw" Him and ate and drank with

Him. Try to wrap your mind around that one! I'd like a reservation at that table. The men on the road to Emmaus, after Jesus' resurrection, had a similar experience; in their case, Jesus didn't eat but offered food to them. While eating, their eyes were opened, and they identified the stranger as the resurrected Jesus. Luke 24:13–35.

Moses is one of the few people in history who got so close to seeing God the Father. God hid him in the cleft of the rock so Moses wouldn't see His face and die. What an encounter! But he was allowed to see His glory. Exodus 33:20–23. You might say it was simultaneously a near-life and a near-death experience.

God, preincarnate YHWH, also appeared to Joshua, Samuel, Gideon, Isaiah, Jeremiah, Zechariah, Balaam, David, Solomon, and other Old Testament characters. Sometimes, He appeared as an Angel of the Lord. Sometimes, He appeared as the "Word of the Lord," as He did to Jeremiah. Sometimes as a cloud, fire, or the Rock that followed them. Often, the Lord would speak to Moses in his tent while encased in a cloud.

The Great I AM: YHWH in the New Testament

All the Old Testament appearances of YHWH telescope into the New Testament and form a direct correlation to YHWH in both Testaments. Seven times in the New Testament, Jesus referred to Himself as "I AM," the equivalent of the Old Testament word *YHWH*.

You are familiar with these declarations:

- I AM the Bread of Life—John 6:35
- I AM the Light of the World—John 8:12; 9:5

- I AM the Door—John 10:7–9
- I AM the Good Shepherd—John 10:11, 14
- I AM the Resurrection and the Life—John 11:25
- I AM the Truth the Life and the Way—John 14:6
- I AM the True Vine—John 15:1

When you read these names, try substituting YHWH, as it will help you to connect the revelation of Jesus as the I AM (YHWH) in both Testaments, for example, "YHWH, the Bread of Life."

There are several other occasions when Jesus referred to Himself as I AM. I'll mention a few of these: John 4:26; 6:20, 51; 8:18, 24, 28, 58; 10:7, 9, 11, 14; 11:25; 13:19; 14:6; 18:5–6, 8. In many translations, it will say, "I am He," but the word *He* is missing in Greek. Jesus merely says, "I AM," which means YHWH. Jesus unequivocally declared Himself to be the YHWH of the Old Testament. The Jews of the day knew what Jesus was calling Himself and were outraged.

My favorite example is in John 18:6 when the soldiers and Judas came to arrest Jesus. *"Whom do you seek?"* Jesus asked. The soldiers answered Him, *"Jesus of Nazareth."* When Jesus answered, *"I am He,"* He identified Himself as "I AM," meaning YHWH. At this, the soldiers drew back and fell to the ground. Jesus is the Great I AM!

Paul's encounter with I AM in Acts 9 brought a similar response. Not only did Paul fall to the ground, but the brightness of Jesus' effulgence blinded him for three days. That's what I call being slain in the Spirit!

When I AM appeared as the slain Lamb in Revelation 5:8, the four living creatures and the twenty-four elders also fell. If you search the book of Revelation, you will notice they fell quite often. As soon as the Lamb made His appearance, they'd fall. I'm sure when I see I AM, that will also be my reaction.

From time immemorial, when people of lesser rank came into the presence of royalty, they bowed down. One day, we will come into the presence of His Majesty, the King of Kings and Lord of Lords. We will fall at His feet and worship Him—no little curtsy or tip of the hat for the saints. The legs give out, and down we go. Again, and again.

Those who rejected the Messiah will one day be forced to bow down. Coercion will not be needed for the saints. When we meet Jesus for the first time, I doubt our bodies will be physically capable of remaining upright. All strength will be gone with one glimpse of His Majesty. We will be crushed under the weight of His glory. Words of gratitude will stick in our mouths like cotton before we can utter them.

If there is any doubt that the I AM of the New Testament is the I AM of the Old Testament, in the gospel of John, Jesus made it unambiguously clear that He was the one who revealed Himself to Abraham as the "I AM." *"Before Abraham was, I AM"* (John 8:58).

If Jesus refers to Himself as I AM (YHWH) in the New Testament, what is to make us think that out of the 6,820 references to YHWH in the Old Testament, many, or even most, of them might not be referring to the preincarnate Jesus as well?

Another revelation of Jesus in the Old Testament is when He is identified as the LORD of Hosts. God the

Father, the invisible YHWH, is never referred to in the Bible as the LORD of Hosts. The General of God's army is always Jesus, whether in the Old or New Testaments. God never leads His armies. That responsibility has been assigned to His Son. Jesus, YHWH, God's Son, is the Captain of the hosts of the Lord.

The Hebrew word for *hosts is* צָבָא, pronounced tsaw-BAW, and it means *armies*. When Jesus returns, as recorded in Revelation 19, He will lead an army of angels and saints.

The Lord of Hosts (Sabaoth) is mentioned only twice in the New Testament, James 5:4 and Romans 9:29, and both Scriptures identify the Captain of Armies (Hosts) as Jesus.

It is clear from Joshua's response in Joshua 5 that the Captain of the LORD's Army was the visible God Himself, YHWH. Bowing in worship before the Captain of the Hosts, who had drawn His sword, Joshua obeyed the command to remove his sandals. Such a command is reserved only for the worship of deity. The fact that the ground is holy further indicates that Joshua's visiting Commander was none other than Jesus preincarnate. It must have been quite an introduction when Joshua met Jesus, whose name in Hebrew is Joshua. "Hey, Joshua, it's me! I, too, am called Joshua. I'm the one with the sword."

Further testimony of Jesus in the Old Testament is found in John 12:41, which emphatically states that Isaiah's vision of the Exalted Lord in Isaiah 6 was none other than Jesus. Another way you can confirm that the LORD of Isaiah 6 is preincarnate Jesus is that He is called the "LORD of hosts." *"Holy, Holy, Holy, is the LORD of hosts* [tsaw-BAW]." Only preincarnate Jesus is referred to as the LORD of Hosts.

NOTE: The only other time "Holy, Holy, Holy" is mentioned in this triad form of praise is in Revelation 4:8, which refers to the Father. Only the Father and the Son are given this reverential treatment.

"Holy, holy, holy, is the LORD of hosts [tsaw-BAW]; *the whole earth is full of his glory!"* (Isaiah 6:3).

"Holy, holy, holy, is the Lord God Almighty, who was and is and is to come" (Revelation 4:8).

On both occasions, the six-winged seraphim give the eternal paean of praise begun in eternity past and extending to eternity future. We will soon join the chorus. I can hardly wait to raise my voice with the redeemed of the ages.

Jesus, Angel of the Lord

Another identifiable presentation of preincarnate Jesus is when the Scriptures mention the Angel of the Lord. Because the definition of angel is *messenger* (*malak* in Hebrew), it's easy to confuse who the messenger is. The Angel of the Lord is Jesus preincarnate. The Father often sent His Son to deliver a personal message, and you'll find Him in many places in the Old Testament. Some of the Old Testament angelic visitations were to Abraham, Jacob, Gideon, Joshua, Hagar, and the mother of Samson.

The most important revelation of Jesus in the Old Testament is His personal leadership in Israel's deliverance from Egypt and their subsequent journey to the Promised Land. He is the God of Israel, just as He is the Head of the church in the New Testament. The Old Testament calls Him Israel's Husband.

"Now I want to remind you, although you know everything once and for all, that Jesus, having saved the people out of the land

of Egypt, the second time destroyed those who did not believe" (Jude v 5).

Note that Jude called Jesus the one who delivered Israel from Egypt. This is a reference from Exodus 23:20–22:

"Behold, I send an angel before you to guard you on the way and to bring you to the place that I have prepared. Pay careful attention to him and obey his voice; do not rebel against him, for he will not pardon your transgression, for my name is in him. But if you carefully obey his voice and do all that I say, then I will be an enemy to your enemies and an adversary to your adversaries."

An additional corroborating voice that the Angel of the Lord is Jesus preincarnate, and the God of Israel is found in Judges 2:1–2:

"Now the angel of the LORD went up from Gilgal to Bochem. And he said, 'I brought you into the land that I swore to give to your fathers. I said, "I will never break my covenant with you, and you shall make no covenant with the inhabitants of this land; you shall break down their altars." But you have not obeyed my voice. What is this you have done?'"

It's important that you see how integrally YHWH, preincarnate Jesus, was involved in the history of Israel, beginning with His appearance to Moses, His giving of the Law, His deliverance from Egypt, and His entrance into the Promised Land. Every element of the wilderness experience has the fingerprints of Jesus showing Himself as the visible YHWH:

The cloud that led them.

The fire that hovered over them.

The rock that followed them.

The rock that poured forth water.

The eighty days of conversations with Moses on Mount Sinai and at his tent of meeting.

Eating with the seventy elders.

The tabernacle, furniture, and sacrificial rituals.

The raised serpent in the wilderness.

The manna they ate for forty years.

The ark of the covenant and the mercy seat.

The blood of the sacrificial animals.

The scapegoat sent into the wilderness.

The lamb slain on Passover and the Day of Atonement.

The voice and presence in the burning bush.

The revelation to Moses as I AM.

The angel of His presence that went with them.

The carrier and conveyor of "the Name."

It is Jesus, Jesus, Jesus—the same Jesus in the New Testament as in the Old Testament. He is the same yesterday, today, and forever (Hebrews 13:8).

It is no mistake that when it was time for Jesus to make His exodus at Calvary, He invited Moses to be one of His two guests on the mountain of Transfiguration. The story is recorded in Luke 9:30–31. Their conversation, according to my translation, centered around His departure. But the Greek doesn't say *departure*. It says *exodus*. Jesus, Moses, and Elijah had all experienced an exodus. Moses and Jesus led one, and Elijah experienced one when chariots and horses of fire carried him to the presence of God.

The Importance of YHWH: Upper and Lower Case Explained

The translators of the Old Testament didn't do us any favors when instead of printing the word *YHWH*, the most common name for God in the Old Testament, they substituted it with the word *LORD* in all capital letters.

Unfortunately, they also used the word *Lord*, but printed with lowercase letters, to mean a completely different name for God—A*donai*, or *Adon*. Though the words *LORD* and *Lord* sound the same, they are printed differently and can mean different persons of the Godhead. The *Lord* (lowercase) can mean a master or ruler.

To help you understand, allow me to show you an example. An easy Scripture to note the difference is in Psalm 110:1: *"The **LORD** says to my **Lord**: 'Sit at my right hand, until I make your enemies your footstool'"* (emphasis added). Notice the difference in the letter cases. The first mention of *Lord* is spelled with all capital letters, *LORD*, while the second uses lower case, *Lord*.

In Psalm 110:1, it's easy to differentiate which Godhead member the writer refers to. The first *LORD* (in all capitals) is the word *YHWH* in Hebrew, referring to God the Father. When the small case, *Lord*, is used, it means *Adon* and refers to Jesus the Son. How do we know? The Scripture is fulfilled in the New Testament. Jesus quotes the first part of the psalm in Matthew 22:44, Mark 12:36, and Luke 20:42–43. The second part of the psalm is quoted in Hebrews 1:13, where the writer says, *"And to which of the angels has he ever said, 'Sit at my right hand until I make your enemies a footstool for your feet.'?"*

In my research, *YHWH* in the Old Testament mainly refers to Jesus as the visible, preincarnate YHWH. The text makes it clear when it is used of the Father, the invisible YHWH, as in Psalm 110:1. Both Father and Son are called

YHWH, meaning I AM, in the Old Testament. The context or text often will clarify which member of the Godhead it is talking about.

Remember, *YHWH* is used six thousand eight hundred times in the Old Testament, but you must identify it by distinguishing between all capital letters and the lowercase. If it is written in capital letters, *LORD*, it is the Hebrew consonants, *YHWH*, meaning *I AM*. If it is written *Lord*, in lower case, it means *Adon*, or *master*.

The intent of this chapter is not to parse words but to bring to our attention that Jesus is the center of the entire Bible and the focal point of our preaching.

Preach Jesus Christ

We must stop preaching a watered-down, compromised gospel and preach Jesus Christ and Him crucified. We must preach Jesus in the context of the Bible, from Genesis to Revelation, and not just the Jesus of the Gospels. The God who walked and talked with Abraham is also the glorified Lord in blinding effulgence in the book of Revelation. People need to know He who was, who is, and who is to come. The Great I AM!

At the end of the age, every knee will bow, and every tongue will confess that Jesus Christ is Lord, to the glory of God the Father (Philippians 2:10). Before the day when every knee shall bow, we MUST:

Teach Christ

Preach Christ

Praise Christ

Declare Christ

Extol Christ

Exalt Christ

Magnify Christ

Love Christ

Obey Christ

Glorify Christ.

Jesus must be Lord of all or nothing at all; there is no middle ground. We must preach Jesus first and foremost.

ABOUT THE AUTHOR

Larry Titus is a spiritual father to multitudes. He has helped men step into their greatness. His family is exemplary and he has led five congregations in his sixty years of ministry. He is the founder and president of Kingdom Global Ministries and is an author and speaker. He lives in the Dallas/Ft Worth Metroplex. Connect with him at KingdomGlobal.com

www.ingramcontent.com/pod-product-compliance
Lightning Source LLC
Chambersburg PA
CBHW052126270326
41930CB00012B/2772